Praise for *Reversing Dyslexia*

"The best investment you will ever make!"

"*Reversing Dyslexia* is the best investment you will ever make as a parent, educator, or therapist of a child with dyslexia. This will be life changing for you and your child! As a parent and a speech pathologist, I have found Dr. Books a resource without equal. Since seeing my own daughter's transformation, I have been referring patients to Dr. Books for years, witnessing success after success in the alleviation of dyslexia. All parents can now experience real hope that their child's diagnosis of dyslexia can be reversed. This book addresses the neurological root of the problem and may even allow you to eliminate time-consuming, frustrating, and costly remedial measures. This is the future of dyslexia intervention."

Ellen Adams, M.Ed., CCC-SLP
Speech-Language Pathologist

"This labor of love was written for us!"

"Dr. Books courageously leads the reader on a journey that challenges and expands the concept of traditional medicine— a journey of hope and perseverance. Parents, educators, physicians, healthcare providers, individuals and families dealing with dyslexia: This labor of love was written for us! *Reversing Dyslexia* is scientifically based, integrative, holistic, and practical—woven together with heart, humor, and a determination to deal with root causes rather than symptoms. Is dyslexia reversible? As Dr. Books would say, 'Come into my office and decide for yourself.'"

Joyce Beck, ACSW, LMSW-ACP
Co-founder of the Crossings, a r   ive
learning center, wellness spa,

REVERSING DYSLEXIA

IMPROVING LEARNING & BEHAVIOR WITHOUT DRUGS

DR. PHYLLIS BOOKS

SQUAREONE
PUBLISHERS

COVER DESIGNER: Jeannie Tudor
EDITOR: Michael Weatherhead
TYPESETTER: Gary A. Rosenberg

Square One Publishers
115 Herricks Road
Garden City Park, NY 11040
(516) 535-2010 • (877) 900-BOOK
www.squareonepublishers.com

Library of Congress Cataloging-in-Publication Data

Books, Phyllis.
  Reversing dyslexia / Phyllis Books, DC, CCN.
    pages cm
  Includes bibliographical references and index.
  ISBN 978-0-7570-0378-3
    1. Dyslexic children—Rehabilitation. 2. Dyslexic children—Education.
3. Dyslexia. 4. Reading disability—Treatment. I. Title.
  RJ496.A5B67 2013
  618.92'8553—dc23
                                        2013009664

Contents

Acknowledgments

No man is an island and no book is created in isolation. I am so thankful to all the people who helped me along the extensive journey of writing this book.

Before I learned to read, which was before I started formal schooling, my mother, a teacher herself, nurtured the growth of my brain through nature, music, and art. My father, the first dyslexic I ever knew, colored my life in ways no schooling could have. Kudos also to so many of my school teachers, who gave generously and made learning come alive. Clarence Imislund, Ms. Cahill, and Sydney Wright guided me through the maze of junior high in the city. Mrs.Chatterson, Pearl Landfair, Bruce Paulson, and Mr. Weber did the same at the high school level—extraordinary teachers, all of them.

Pioneers in various fields have been a guiding light to me: Jean Houston, who breathed the possibilities of unlimited potential into her myriad of students; Elaine De Beauport, who mentored me in the ways of accessing and healing various parts of the brain; Fritjof Capra, who made modern physics come to life; Don Campbell, departed friend and colleague, who shared his vast knowledge of music and healing; Charles Krebs, affectionately known as Chuckopedia, who gave me access to his encyclopedic knowledge and awareness of brain facts both great and small;

Carla Hannaford, who dissected the neurophysiology of learning into bite-size chunks; Bertrand deJarnette, who developed Sacro Occipital Technique; Ted Morter, who developed Bio Energetic Synchronization Technique; Donny Epstein, who ushered in Network Spinal Analysis; Carl Ferreri, who created Neural Organization Therapy; George Goodheart, who brought Applied Kinesiology to the word; John Thie, who took Applied Kinesiology to the larger audience via Touch for Health; Paul Dennison, who developed Brain Gym; John Upledger, who dared to spread the knowledge of craniosacral work beyond the field of osteopathy; Richard Bandler and John Grinder, who studied the work of Erik Erikson and Virginia Satir and birthed Neuro-Linguistic Programming; Roger Callahan and Gary Craig, who exposed the world to Emotional Freedom Technique; and Scott and Deb Walker, who championed Neuro Emotional Technique. These people all left their thumbprints on my life.

Thanks to my publisher, Rudy Shur, for believing in me and forcing me to dig into uncharted territories within myself to bring forth this book; and to Michael Weatherhead, my editor, who was a gentlemen and a scholar, always treating me with great respect and a light touch. Bernice Dotz, my "business mom," deserves special acknowledgement for believing in me and relentlessly cajoling me to write this book and develop the teaching curriculum.

The biggest teachers come to me daily in the form of children and parents. Thank you for allowing me access into the deep places within you, where pain and misunderstanding are lodged. You are my teachers and inspiration. My children, grandchildren, and extended family nourish me, fill me with unconditional love and support, and give me a safe place to recharge. Love heals; and the love I feel from my family allows me to extend a loving hand to others.

Foreword

It is my great pleasure to write the foreword to such an important work as *Reversing Dyslexia*. As a physician who practices integrative medicine, I am often called upon to tackle the hardest cases— the ones in which all other doctors have failed. Sadly, dyslexia and other learning behaviors typically fit into this category, but why? In my opinion, dyslexia is not an incurable disease. I feel the same holds true for pervasive developmental disorders (PDD) such as autism, as well as for other neurological syndromes that have been written off by mainstream medicine as conditions that patients must endure for the rest of their lives without any chance of improvement. I simply do not believe the popular view of these problems.

While there have been several books and many theories on autism and its rising case numbers, there has not been a very good text on dyslexia until now. In her book, Dr. Books does an amazing job teaching the reader that dyslexia does not necessarily need to last forever. While explaining the science behind this idea in an uncomplicated and relatable way, Dr. Books convincingly supports the notion that the human brain never stops learning or changing. She then shrewdly acknowledges that it is actually possible to rewire the neural pathways of the brain to help in the fight against dyslexia.

Astoundingly, this simple reality has been ignored by educational systems, medical schools, and the pharmaceutical industry. Traditional medical doctors and practitioners seem simply unable to grasp the fact that there are, in fact, ways to turn even the most complicated learning disorder around. Modern medicine does not encourage patients to take power over their learning issues and control of their lives; it only labels them. Once a label sticks, it is hard to remove. It may even become a defense mechanism, stripping an individual of self-worth and discouraging any effort to change. Fortunately, many people are now turning away from the mainstream medical approach to dyslexia and looking at other options. They no longer wish to remain hopeless, and they do not need to remain so. There are alternative, natural therapies that can heal issues of the brain and central nervous system. Through the use of these methods, dyslexia may be eliminated at the level of causation, becoming a thing of the past.

The point of this book is to declare the elimination of dyslexia a very real possibility. In doing so, *Reversing Dyslexia* is a true breakthrough work. Dyslexia is not simply having difficulty with reading and writing. It is a disorder that permeates a person's entire life, promoting all sorts of unwanted symptoms, from poor organizational skills to behavior and attitude problems. Thanks to the information outlined by Dr. Books, lives may be changed for the better. When a healer follows the natural order of the body and looks at the deepest levels of development, only then may true restoration can take place. *Reversing Dyslexia* proves Dr. Books to be such a healer. I learned a lot from this important work and so will you.

Fred Pescatore, MD, MPH, CCN

Preface

I embrace the beautiful but tattered souls of my young patients every day as we do our reading, writing, marching, and physical activities together. Dyslexic children come to me with broken hearts, lacking confidence and wondering if they will ever be able to learn like other kids. Most of these children are burdened by a sense of shame, wilting from the fear of disappointing their parents, their teachers, and themselves. Dyslexia keeps them down, their talents trapped beneath a mountain of humiliation.

The label of dyslexia can become a painful cloak to wear day in and day out. It can kill a child's motivation and creativity. Watching a child's innocence and joy be replaced by hesitation, embarrassment, and defeat breaks a parent's heart. Parents don't want to fail or give up on their children. Doing so would go against the deepest parental instinct, which is to nourish and protect the young.

I understand firsthand how the spirit of a child can be crushed by a learning disorder. Thankfully, I also know the incredibly freeing and empowering experience of watching a child overcome such obstacles—the feeling that says, "I did this! Today I am king of the mountain. I really am in charge of my life and I really can create the life I want. What else have I been told is impossible but really isn't?" My desire to bring this experience to others led me to write this book.

I wrote this book to dispel the myth that dyslexia is permanent. The idea that learning disorders are unchangeable is simply untrue, and it harms children. It affects relationships and families, and undermines productivity and the ability to make a living. As a society of taxpayers, we are all paying the price of this mistaken idea in one way or another. I also wrote this book to open minds to a new way of looking at dyslexia, to create empowered advocates for dyslexic kids, and to make sure individuals get the help they need to dismantle the problem of dyslexia for good. Most of all, I wrote this book to help free the human spirit—the spirit that still lives inside every dyslexic person and begs to be unchained.

Introduction

When a child has dyslexia, reading troubles and other associated problems can become overwhelming, and the prognosis from the educational and medical world can be discouraging at best. Popular opinion states that dyslexia is permanent—a problem for which you must learn to compensate—and that you should not believe anyone who says otherwise. *Reversing Dyslexia* proposes a different view—one that may very well include a happy ending. As the title suggests, dyslexia, in fact, may be reversible. In addition, when dyslexia is eliminated, many of its accompanying issues, including poor organization, poor time management, and low self-esteem, may be lessened or erased as well. I say all this with confidence because I've seen it happen. I've watched children who once hated reading devour books after the obstacles of dyslexia were removed. And these success stories are not just about academic improvement. I've read notes from soccer and football coaches expressing their amazement at children's athletic ability after therapy. I've received phone calls years after treatment from parents so grateful that their kids didn't end up in jail, on drugs, or even institutionalized—parents who were close to giving up, who did not know where to turn or what to believe.

Throughout my quarter century as an educator, chiropractor, and nutritionist, I have worked with thousands of children in many countries and instructed healthcare providers on three continents. I have seen dyslexic children go back to mainstream classes, get college degrees, and achieve fulfilling careers. I know that dyslexia is reversible because I have witnessed this change over and over again. You too may be able to witness it, but not before you embrace a new mindset. You have to believe change is possible. I know you don't want to get your hopes up. I know you've been disappointed so many times. I'm asking you not to give up. This book presents important information on dyslexia in a logical, step-by-step, practical way that will allow you to see for yourself that change is possible.

Because dyslexia is always so narrowly and inappropriately defined, Chapter 1 seeks to clarify this condition by redefining it in broader terms. It explains the various theories of dyslexia and considers the fact that each of these theories may be valid in its own way. It then details the possible causes of dyslexia, from genetic predispositions to environmental reasons. Chapter 2 aims to help you determine whether or not your child is dyslexic. It not only describes the common clues that point to this issue, which include symptoms such as difficulty reading and trouble remembering oral instructions, but also lists associated conditions that parents may overlook as markers of dyslexia, including ADHD, depression, and anxiety. To adjust the established view of dyslexia and change the traditional approach to therapy, Chapter 3 sheds light on the Triune Brain, which divides the brain into three layers. This idea of a three-tiered system suggests that therapy must begin at the lowest level of the brain and move upwards in order to be truly successful. It also illustrates how important the notions of safety, attachment, physical movement, and creativity are to cognitive development and learning.

Chapter 4 calls into question the traditional approaches to therapy, which mostly rely on workarounds and compensatory measures, by explaining the scientific studies of neuroplasticity and epigenetics. These fields consistently show how the brain may be rewired at any age—an idea that holds great significance to the reversal of dyslexia and other learning challenges. It goes on to outline alternative treatments that may help to retrain the brain, and offers information that can effectively guide you in treatment decisions. Chapter 5 describes the huge role nutrition plays in learning and learning disorders, focusing on the four major sources of trouble: wheat, dairy, sugar, and caffeine. It also explains how to change your mindset about food and improve the quality of every meal you have, including snacks.

Building on the idea of layered brain development and the possibility of rewiring the brain, Chapter 6 discusses the three major brain boosters: exercise, music, and play. It gives examples of all sorts of activities you can do at home to promote a fully integrated brain and stimulate the ability to learn easily. Finally, Chapter 7 details the schooling options available at every level and suggests which ones may be the most beneficial to a dyslexic individual. This information will help you make the informed choices necessary to ensure an advantageous learning environment. This chapter also considers the benefits of tutoring and recommends helpful extracurricular activities to pursue throughout the school year and during summer break.

New science strongly suggests that a family history of dyslexia doesn't mean you must suffer from this learning disorder as well. *Reversing Dyslexia* describes how previously controversial approaches to treatment are now being scientifically validated. The right combination of therapy and at-home practices can make an immense difference in the life of a dyslexic individual.

Dyslexia and all its connected problems often feel like more than one person can manage, so I hope that you consider me a partner in your struggle as you read this book. The label of dyslexia is a difficult one to wear, but it does not have to be a permanent mark. The brain can change. Dyslexia is not necessarily destiny.

1.

Getting to the Roots of Dyslexia

A s a little girl, I spent a lot of time with a thermometer under my tongue waiting for the doctor to make yet another house call. One particular day, when my mother tried coaxing it into my mouth for the umpteenth time, I rebelled and bit the device into two pieces. To my amazement, a little blob of mercury rolled out of the broken thermometer and onto the floor. The shiny silver form immediately fascinated me. When I probed and poked it, it changed shapes easily. I couldn't scoop it up in my hands. I couldn't put it back into the broken thermometer, into a jar, or even into my pocket. It was slippery and evasive. It was elusive and hard to contain.

Dyslexia is a bit like that mercury—hard to pin down and difficult to control. Just when you think you've got it figured out, cornered, or harnessed, it seems to change shape, escape, and reappear somewhere else. One of the trickiest parts of dyslexia is simply figuring out what it is. Curiously, neither researchers, nor educators, nor any group of experts can seem to agree on a definition of dyslexia. Without an accurate definition, how can we understand and remedy this mysterious problem? Let me assure you that dyslexia is definable and, in most cases, reversible.

We can achieve a better and fuller understanding of dyslexia. To do so, we must begin with an overview of dyslexia's origin and history. We must also become familiar with the numerous interpretations of dyslexia to see why this condition has confounded people for so long. By learning the many theories surrounding dyslexia, we will see why the problem has been so hard to pin down. By reading about the symptoms and conditions often associated with dyslexia —many of which are not related to reading at all—we will recognize the need to adopt a new and more comprehensive definition of this issue. By considering the possible causes of this disorder, we may see it in a new light. It is only by getting to the roots of dyslexia that we may be able to reverse it.

DEFINING DYSLEXIA

Dyslexia is a relatively modern problem because reading as we know it is a fairly new development in human history. Humans are biologically hardwired to speak and listen. In fact, a human fetus's ears are fully developed by the sixth month of pregnancy. It is important to note, however, that although humans are naturally designed to speak and hear, we are *not* naturally designed to read. Reading, or the act of deciphering symbols and assigning them sounds and meaning, was invented by humans.

Although the term *dyslexia* was coined in 1887, it didn't come into common usage until the 1960s. It is derived from the Greek root words *dys*, which means "abnormal" or "impaired," and *lexis*, which means "words" or "speech." While dyslexia is generally considered a reading disability, the fact that it can manifest itself in a number of different ways makes it difficult to describe accurately using such a narrow and simplistic definition. Some dyslexics transpose the words in a sentence or reverse the letters of a word, such as seeing a "b" as a "d." Some see reverse images of numbers. For others, distracting splotches of color appear on the page. Simply keeping written letters and words the same size and maintaining the same spacing between letters and words can be troublesome. Words or letters may jump around or slide off the page. They may even become blurry, grow in size, or shrink.

In defining dyslexia, however, it must be noted that this condition can be much more than a simple reading problem. It is frequently associated with other symptoms. Spoken words may come out all mixed up, with words or phrases occurring in the wrong sequence within a sentence. Reading aloud may sound jerky and uneven in rhythm. Remembering words and facts from day to day, or even moment to moment, may be inconsistent. Physical issues are also quite common. Dyslexics may display an uneven gait, walking pigeon-toed or with one foot splayed out. Other issues linked to dyslexia include:

- hand-eye coordination problems and poor motor skills

- inability to focus or concentrate

- low self-esteem or distorted self-image

- poor sense of direction (often confusing right and left)

- problems carrying out multiple instructions

- behavioral issues

- delayed response (frequently requiring a phrase to be repeated)

- difficulty making decisions

A person can exhibit one or more of the previously mentioned traits without having dyslexia, of course. If dyslexia *is* an issue, though, a number of these signs are likely to accompany it.

THEORIES OF DYSLEXIA

There are several schools of thought when it comes to dyslexia, and people from different professional backgrounds tend to see the problem through their own filters. From the perspective of most educators, it's purely a reading and spelling recognition issue. To occupational and physical therapists, it's a sensory integration issue. To audiologists and sound therapists, it's an auditory issue. To vision therapists, it's a visual perception issue. From chiropractic, osteopathic, and naturopathic viewpoints, it stems from various imbalances within the body. While the existence of so many differing views makes the issue of dyslexia harder to pin down, these theories collectively show how multifaceted the problem actually is.

Due to a history of researchers and experts focusing on only one aspect of dyslexia, a complete picture of this condition seems to be missing. Without a complete picture, the many factors at play in dyslexics may be overlooked. When dealing with the current explanations of dyslexia, the old saying "you can't see the forest for the trees" often applies. It helps to step back and look at every possibility.

Phonological Deficit Theory

This theory characterizes dyslexia as a breakdown between the smallest unit of written language, also known as a *grapheme*, and the basic unit of spoken language, also known as a *phoneme*. According to this theory, dyslexics cannot link the sounds (phonemes) of speech to their symbolic representations (graphemes). Essentially, the sounds of letters are poorly represented and stored in the brain, resulting in a problem with grapheme-phoneme correspondence when reading. This theory, however, does not account for the sensory disorders (auditory and visual) or the motor disorders found in many dyslexics.

Rapid Auditory Processing Theory

A more specific version of the phonological deficit theory, this explanation paints dyslexia as a failure to correctly discriminate short or rapidly varying sounds, which leads to the problem of grapheme-phoneme correspondence mentioned in the phonological deficit theory.

Visual Theory

Probably the most common and traditional view of dyslexia, visual theory focuses on the inability to process visual information from letters and words on a page. The visual impairment causes trouble discerning the order of letters in a word and the sequence of words in a sentence. This theory does not exclude phonological issues that may also accompany the main visual problem.

Cerebellar Theory

Located at the base of the skull, the cerebellum is part of the brainstem. Shaped like a small cauliflower and nicknamed "the little brain," the cerebellum has long been known to coordinate "lower brain" motor skills, balance, and muscle tone. Thanks to research involving new, sophisticated methods of measurement, there is now evidence that it also plays a crucially important role in many "higher brain" functions, including language and attention. The cerebellar theory puts forth the idea that a low-functioning cerebellum can lead to dyslexia.

According to this theory, a dysregulated cerebellum can negatively affect the motor function of speech articulation, leading to phonological problems and dyslexia. It can also disrupt the automatization of various tasks, including driving, typing, and reading. An inability to make certain practices automatic can adversely affect the process of learning grapheme-phoneme correspondence.

While brain scans have shown cerebellar differences in dyslexics, this theory fails to explain the absence of motor dysfunction in many dyslexics. It also includes the debunked link between speech articulation and phonological difficulties. (There are many cases of normal phonological function in people with pronounced speech impediments.)

Magnocellular Theory

Magnocellular cells are part of the visual system, and the magnocellular theory of dyslexia stems from the visual theory. The magnocellular model, however, suggests that dysfunction in these cells may not affect only visual networks, but also auditory and motor functions. Basically, it proposes one biological cause of every deficit that has been linked to dyslexia. Although it is a tempting explanation, it too has its problems. Primarily, researchers have not been able to display the presence of auditory, visual, and motor disorders in all dyslexics. In addition, the mere idea of magnocellular cells affecting nonvisual systems is still very controversial and not universally accepted.

Naming Speed Deficit and Double Deficit Theories

Naming speed deficit theory postulates that the speed with which a person is able to name aloud familiar objects or letters can be a reliable predictor of dyslexia, with slower speeds being associated with this condition. This theory was devised to differentiate the problem from a phonological deficit, which is an important distinction when it comes to treatment. Double deficit theory states that people who exhibit both a naming speed deficit and a phonological disorder are even more likely to be dyslexic.

Scotopic Sensitivity Syndrome (Irlen Syndrome)

Scotopic Sensitivity Syndrome (SSS), also known as Irlen Syndrome, deals with a kind of dyslexia in which words seem to move or jump around on the page during the reading process. According to SSS, the problem is the result of a lack of integration of certain neural pathways and can be remedied by special lenses that filter specific colors from the light spectrum. When a person affected with this type of dyslexia wears theses lenses, the issue seems to disappear.

Perceptual Visual-Noise Exclusion Hypothesis

Some researchers hypothesize that dyslexia results from the impaired filtration of unnecessary visual and auditory information. Extraneous visual and auditory "noise" can distract people who are incapable of distinguishing what is important from what is irrelevant. Concentration becomes comprised and reading difficult.

Evolutionary Hypothesis

As stated at the outset of this chapter, reading is a relatively modern development. Humans have been decoding abstract symbols that visually represent speech for only a few thousand years. We are preprogrammed to hear and speak, but not to read. Adaptation and mutation, which are considered signs of intelligence and survival in evolutionary theory, take time—often many generations. Some researchers view dyslexia as evidence that humanity simply hasn't adapted fully into a reading species yet. In addition, some see the rapidly changing technology of the digital world as making this adaptation even harder. Many neurological glitches or timing issues may occur when various systems of the body cannot integrate changes fast enough, possibly leading to dyslexia.

CAUSES OF DYSLEXIA

The numerous and differing explanations for dyslexia seem to make the disorder even harder to understand and treat. I believe, however, that a broader and more comprehensive view of the problem is necessary to solve it, so multiple points of view may be beneficial. One theory or hypothesis need not be completely correct or absolutely wrong. Perhaps these various approaches to dyslexia are each valid in some way, successfully treating subtypes of what should be known as general dyslexia. Even in connection with the most basic reading comprehension issues, the many building blocks and stages of development that prepare the body to function normally should be addressed.

I have found that the reading problem of dyslexia is often the culmination of earlier issues not being resolved; it is the tip of the iceberg, so to speak. This open-minded approach should be taken not only when figuring out the process behind a patient's dyslexia, but also when considering the cause of this process. In my twenty-five years of clinical experience, I have found that there are several causes of dyslexia, and that many of these causes fall outside traditional views. While genetics can definitely be responsible for this disorder, the effects that nurture and environment can have on a person may also reveal origins of dyslexia not yet considered. As an alternative and complementary medicine doctor, I find that looking at the larger picture often provides crucial information.

Genetics

Some experts claim that dyslexia is a genetic problem, possibly beginning in utero. Biologically, we know that the ear and sense of hearing are fully developed at six months after conception. Hearing and listening are involved in decoding words and sounds, which are necessary skill sets involved in reading. If there is interference in the proper development of these senses, reading—as well as balance, synchronization, and timing—can affect learning.

Genetic brain chemistry imbalances may also cause dyslexia, such as when neurotransmitters do not work properly. Neurotransmitters are messengers that carry information from one area of the brain to another. If they misfire and send information to the wrong place, or if there is too much of one chemical and not enough of another, the brain can't do its job. Incorrect timing and poor integration of the parts of the brain can result in faulty processing. When signals are weak or fuzzy, the maps that are laid down in the brain for future learning have the same fuzzy signature. When these brain chemicals are out of balance, behaviors such as obsessive-compulsive behavior, anger issues, rapid mood swings, and depression can take hold. The brain can be caught in a vicious loop, unable to self-correct until its chemistry is brought back into balance. Thankfully, now that we have more comprehensive and detailed versions of x-rays and brain scans, we are also learning natural ways of changing the wiring of the brain. A genetic cause of dyslexia does not mean the disorder cannot be reversed.

Most simply, genetic reasons for dyslexia are supported by the fact that the issue tends to run in families. If one parent is dyslexic, there is a 50-percent chance one of the children will be, too. It is important to note, however, that while genetics likely play a role in many cases of dyslexia, to declare the issue as strictly inborn may not be accurate, and may also foster the untrue belief that dyslexia cannot be eliminated.

Birth Trauma

During the last few weeks before birth, the head of the baby descends and can push against the mother's pelvic bones, most commonly with the left front side of the skull. Interestingly, many problems associated with dyslexia originate from the left side of the brain. In addition, forceps deliveries, where pincers are placed on either side of the baby's head to aid in delivery, can also affect the skull in ways that might lead to dyslexia. In fact, families have won lawsuits filed when forceps-delivered babies later became

A New Life

Ron, a sixty-eight-year-old building contractor, appeared in my office one day asking if I thought I could help someone his age learn to read. "Absolutely," I said. "Age has nothing to do with it." As his story unfolded, I learned that Ron had experienced a very difficult and traumatic birth. According to his mother, Ron came out "all crooked." At his fifty-year class reunion, Ron publicly thanked all his classmates for helping him graduate. If they hadn't helped him cheat, he admitted, he would not have a high school diploma.

In my estimation, Ron's dyslexia was caused by his birth process. By correcting and undoing the physical trauma of birth via gentle movements around the neck and skull, as well as retraining his eye muscles to move in new ways (thus correcting and updating his neurological circuitry), Ron was able to read—finally. A completely new world opened up to him. He burst into my office one day, his eyes all aglow with childlike wonder, and exclaimed, "I'm reading as though I've read all my life."

dyslexic. These days, difficult deliveries use a suction technique instead of forceps. Finally, pulling a baby from the birth canal by the neck, particularly when too much force is used, may result in learning disabilities.

Emotional Trauma

Whenever an emotional trauma occurs, whether it is an isolated incident or repeated, there can be a huge and longstanding impact on the nervous system. It causes a person to fight, flee, or freeze—

Doing the Math

Fourteen-year-old Ken came to my office accompanied by his mother, a school nurse, to address his problems with math. Ken had lost his father at the tender age of seven. He was the youngest of six children, and most of his siblings were living on their own. Ken never cried over the loss of his father and refused to talk to anyone about it, including his mother. He was awfully quiet and didn't have many friends. Despite these troubles, he was doing pretty well in school, except when it came to math.

One day, while Ken and I were working together, I was rubbing my fingertips close to the edges of his eye sockets. Fibrous connective tissue known as *fascia*, which, in this case, was connecting the eye muscles to the bones in Ken's eye sockets, is normally smooth and sinewy. Ken's fascia, however, felt like hard, coarse grains of salt. I knew that this issue could be affecting the muscles and nerves of Ken's eyes, possibly causing interference with visual input and its interpretation. But who would ever think that such emotional scars could be connected to a physical issue that could lead to dyslexia? It was as if the emotional trauma of losing his father had frozen Ken's ocular muscles, inhibiting proper development. With a few therapeutic adjustments of the area around his eyes, Ken was able to improve his math skills. He even began to open up to his mother and move past the emotional grief that had lead to his problems in the first place.

each of which are primitively wired survival tactics that may result when the body is faced with an emergency. In survival mode, the hindbrain, which is reactive, takes over; the forebrain, which thinks ahead, shuts down. Have you ever found yourself upset over what someone said and all of a sudden you can't think straight about anything? Your brain becomes stuck replaying the scene and what you wish you would have said or would still like to say. Emotional trauma and stress can result in all sorts of physical changes, affecting muscles and nerves throughout the body, and disrupting the ability to learn properly.

Concussions

Did you know that you don't have to be knocked unconscious to experience a concussion? What child hasn't fallen out of a crib or high chair, or off a bike? Most of the time a child's body cushions the fall just fine, but sometimes the injury is worse than it seems. Have you ever dropped a dinner plate? Often it just bounces or rolls but remains in one piece. Occasionally, the slightest ding can shatter the dinner plate. The same can occur with people—a blow to the head or tailbone (which is connected to the skull via the spinal cord) can be more serious than it appears, possibly resulting in physical or chemical changes that can have lasting effects on learning ability.

How often does this happen? Not very often. But dyslexia, as you now know, is a complex, multifaceted disorder. It is time to consider all theories and causes of this issue, so that it may be treated according to each individual's needs. Nothing should be dismissed outright or overlooked. When someone receives a blow to the head or tailbone, there is potential for a hairline fracture or a concussion. There are normal tumbles and falls, but don't assume that nothing of consequence happened simply because there was no bleeding or concussion noted. If someone you know has suddenly begun to struggle academically, it's a good idea to ask if this person recently suffered a blow to the head or tailbone.

Sports Injuries and
Their Effect on Learning

Beware of those "headers" in soccer! Jeff was an excellent soccer player, but he also ended up in my office because his life was out of control and his parents were desperate. Once an adorable and smart five-year-old, at seventeen he began to display sudden and violent displays of temper. Mostly he was moody, depressed, and uncooperative. And he had completely stopped trying to read. In the course of talking to Jeff's father, I learned of all the minor head injuries Jeff had experienced while playing soccer, and then I knew what was wrong.

Statistics show that the hormone cortisol, which is triggered by stressful events, increases after a concussion and can stay elevated for years. Likewise, the neurotransmitter serotonin, which helps maintain a positive mood, decreases after head injuries and sometimes stays low. Jeff had no obvious dyslexia at early stages in school, but it was clear that he had stopped reading properly after sustaining a number of concussions. Thankfully, Jeff was able to remedy his dyslexia through a combination of Books Neural Therapy, neurotransmitter testing, allergy desensitization, and biofeedback. (See page 51.) In fact, his parents call me every year around the holidays to remind themselves how much he has changed.

Another example is Tim, a junior in high school whose mother took him for a brain scan after his grades mysteriously dropped. While Tim did not think much of it, he had recently been hit in the head by a baseball, and his mother thought there might be a connection between this incident and his falling test scores. As it turned out, there was a skull injury, and it was likely the reason for his abnormal academic performance. His mom brought him in for biofeedback sessions to treat the issue. At the end of nine weeks, his grades were back up again.

Allergies

At least 75 percent of the time, children who show up in my office with dyslexia also have allergies. Interestingly, handwriting, reading, and behavior can all be affected by allergies. Allergies may not be the main cause of dyslexia, but as you'll recall, there can be many coexisting factors at play when it comes to this disorder. When your body encounters an allergen, its internal organ defenses go up. It's as if an enemy is coming, and the survival part of your brain reports for active duty to fight it off. Your body's natural defenses try to protect you at all costs, but the process may affect learning. When your head is congested and your air passages are blocked, it's hard to get enough oxygen to think clearly.

In addition, as a clinical nutritionist, I often encounter children with food sensitivities that have gone unrecognized but are causing a number of problems. For example, I regularly witness the contribution dairy products make to recurrent ear infections in children. Hearing can be compromised due to ear infections during the formative years when a child is differentiating sounds. According to the famous French physician Dr. Alfred Tomatis, "you can only reproduce sounds you hear." If a child cannot hear all sounds and their nuances, clarity of speech and reading readiness skills can fall behind long before school begins. Parents of a child with frequent ear infections will often consider a regression in the ability to speak clearly a reason to schedule another appointment with the ear doctor, who is likely to prescribe yet another set of ear tubes to drain the accumulated fluid.

Because allergens can provoke physical symptoms and slow down the learning process, many of my educational therapist colleagues suggest that parents address their dyslexic child's allergies *before* trying other therapies.

Nutrition

A child's brain needs the proper fuel to grow and operate efficiently. A good balance of protein, carbohydrates, and fats—and a

A Breath of Fresh Air

A very concerned set of Indian parents brought in their seven-year-old son, Rah, because his school was suggesting he might be autistic. After twenty-five years in the field, I knew I had a pretty good sense of who has what in the world of learning and behavior, and from my observation, Rah was a bright and engaged little fellow with good eye contact and social skills—not typical for autism spectrum disorders. His parents let me know that Rah could barely breathe at night, and that many nights they filled the bathtub with hot, steamy water for Rah to inhale, in the hope that it might clear his sinuses. The traditional medical world wanted him on inhalers and steroids, but Rah's mother wanted to use more natural methods to help him breathe.

I soon discovered that Rah was very allergic to dairy products, including milk, ice cream, yogurt, and cheese. I employed a simple method of desensitizing this allergy, which included tapping various points on the subject's spine and massaging particular points on his arms and legs while he held the allergen. (See page 66.) Children love this approach, as it uses no needles; and I always prefer to use natural, non-invasive ways to coax the brain and nervous system into having a different response to an allergen. Within a week, his mother told me, "This is unbelievable, but he just wrote a story for his class assignment. His handwriting was better and he wrote with better sentence structure and a stronger thought process. Could that be from clearing the allergy?" I said, "Absolutely."

diet that includes many green foods—can help with focus and concentration. Sending a child to school on a breakfast of sugar-coated cereal and juice made with high-fructose corn syrup is a recipe for learning problems. Poor performance at school, on the other hand, can be significantly improved through good nutrition. This may sound preposterous or extreme to you, but I have literally seen high-sugar diets turn A students into F students.

A diet with too much sugar has a physical effect on the body that can be disastrous to learning. One example I see in my office regularly deals with a specific bone in the skull, called the sphe-noid bone. This butterfly-shaped bone forms part of the eye socket. When it is even slightly out of alignment, all thirteen bones it contacts are also affected, distorting vision. Blood sugar levels can even affect the prescription strength of eyeglasses.

The Shocking Effects of Sugar

When eight-year-old Meghan came to see me, she was getting Ds and Fs in all her subjects, and of course, she hated going to school. I started treatment by assessing her strengths and weaknesses, and then designed a set of exercises and therapies that would stimulate her brain's capacity to process the basic information required to read and do math. We did physical coordination exercises to wake up her brain and get the signals firing in the right areas. We did eye exercises together. I performed gentle movements around her eyes and ears to help coordinate neurological pathways and connections between her body and brain.

Within two or three months of our working together, Meghan's father started crowing about his daughter, who was now getting all As and Bs. This lasted almost a year. Then one day, I received a rather frantic call from Meghan's dad, who said his A student was flunking math again. The call came about three weeks after Halloween, so I asked him if Meghan had been eating candy. "Yes," he replied. When she came to see me again, we talked about sugar and how that seemed to be creating a problem with her learning. She literally crawled into the corner, in an almost fetal position, and cried, "I can't live without sugar."

Sugar is a potent and addictive substance, and can actually cause some of the bones that form the eye socket to slide out of place, lead-ing to problems with information processing. (See page 80.) In Meghan's case, it took the removal of excess sugar from her diet and my gently coaxing the bones and muscles around her eye sockets back into their correct positions to remedy her math problem. In a matter of days, she returned to being an A student again.

Processing and interpreting written information then becomes almost impossible to do correctly. Unfortunately, when a child eats too much sugar, the body's reaction can dislodge this bone from its proper position.

Don't get me wrong; the brain runs on sugar, but it should receive its sugar from complex carbohydrates such as legumes, starchy vegetables, and fruit—not refined table sugar, and certainly not the high-fructose corn syrup that is found in practically all packaged foods today.

Finally, the brain also requires fat to run well. In the United Kingdom, during very tough economic times, cod liver oil was doled out to the needy, much like people receive food stamps in the United States. Why cod liver oil? Fish oil is an incredibly rich source of good fat, which is essential for brain function. Healthy fats can also be found in a variety of other foods, including avocados, olive oil, and almonds.

Non-Brain Dominance

Most people are either right-handed or left-handed, but sometimes a person is considered both. This condition is called ambidexterity. Individuals with learning disorders, however, are

Losing to Win

A high school quarterback helped his team win most of their games one year. He could throw the ball equally well with his right or left hand; because of this, he could fake out the other teams. After the coach learned that this quarterback could not read, he had every single football player crawling on his hands and knees the entire length of the football field twice a day. Why did he do that? The coach knew that developing eye dominance begins with the eyes moving from left to right during the crawling process, and that reading also requires this same left-to-right eye movement. The next season, the quarterback lost his ability to throw equally well with either hand, but he gained the ability to read.

often found to be non-ambidextrous, which means being neither right-hand nor left-hand dominant. This is an important distinction. A lack of dominance of one side of the body can result in slowed timing and problems with synchronization, which can interfere with fluent reading.

CONCLUSION

One of the reasons our understanding of dyslexia hasn't really changed in the last century is because we weren't seeing the whole problem. If I had stayed in education, I would never have seen the bigger picture either. It took my leaving the field and becoming a chiropractor—the kind of doctor who focuses on the neuromusculoskeletal system, which includes the brain and spinal cord—to address the questions left unanswered from my teaching training. Dyslexia has been defined in many ways, ranging from simplistic and incomplete to largely academic and difficult to understand. Based on my years of experience and a growing body of scientific information, I feel that dyslexia should be named *dyslexia spectrum syndrome* and defined as:

> A complex neurobiological issue involving brain synchronization and neurological dysregulation, which may appear to varying degrees in relation to reading, math, spelling, physical coordination, memory, and decision making.

Dyslexia is actually a very complex and dynamic situation—far more so than most people recognize—but it can be reversed. To reverse dyslexia and make the act of reading fluid, a solid neurological foundation is essential. Therapists need to address each part of the brain and consider the nervous system as a whole to make sure everything is working as it should. Many seemingly unrelated factors can combine to impact a child's development and behavior. Approaching dyslexia from only one vantage point can be a real disservice to someone with this disorder.

As a condition, dyslexia is certainly more than meets the eye. Although perceptions of dyslexia within the scientific and medical professions vary widely (and are often narrowly focused), this issue is actually layered and multidimensional. In the past, effective solutions have been as elusive as the imbalance itself. In my experience, however, dyslexia is reversible in almost every case, once all the elements involved are uncovered. So have hope. We are just beginning to see dyslexia in a whole new light— a light that will lead the way towards a real solution.

2.

Determining Dyslexia

It's hard to watch your child suffer and not know why or what to do. It is extremely difficult to see your child unable to progress academically, held back by a problem you do not understand or even recognize. It is painful to lie awake at night and wonder if the signs your child has been displaying are indications of dyslexia. No one likes feeling helpless, least of all a parent.

As previously suggested, dyslexia is slippery and hard to pin down. Just as no two people are exactly alike, dyslexia can differ from person to person. The symptoms of this condition can also vary in intensity and severity from day to day. But these facts do not mean all hope is lost. They simply point to the need for information and understanding. They call for a change in perspective and reveal the importance of stepping back and seeing the whole picture. When it comes to diagnosing dyslexia, knowledge is power. The more you know, the better you will be able to recognize and explain your child's particular issues with dyslexia. Once you are able to view the vastness of the issue as a whole, the less likely it will be for someone to pigeonhole your child while ignoring other facets of the issue. You will feel confident to push for treatment that is more comprehensive and, therefore, more successful.

If you are at a loss as to why your child seems unable to meet certain expectations in life, or you already suspect the presence of dyslexia, it is crucial to know the most common signs of this condition and determine if they apply to your child, whether at home or in an academic setting. In addition, it is vital to understand that dyslexia is often associated with other learning problems, including dyscalculia, dysgraphia, dyspraxia, and ADHD. Finally, the psychological and emotional issues that can come with dyslexia must be addressed as parts of the condition as a whole, so that your child isn't simply dismissed as lazy or moody.

The first step in successfully treating dyslexia comes by recognizing that the condition is more than just a reading problem. Dyslexia is not a true disability but rather a learning difference. Understanding the dyslexic brain leads to respecting the dyslexic mind, and this respect will lead to successful treatment.

COMMON CLUES

If your child's progress is lagging but you don't know why, you might want to take a closer look at the possibility of dyslexia. If you already suspect dyslexia, recognizing the signs of this issue may cause you to seek professional evaluation and help you steer your child towards the proper form of treatment. You may see the symptoms of dyslexia both at school and at home. For example, at home your child may:

- deny hearing the beginning or middle of a long speech
- give slow or delayed responses
- have a hard time finding the right word to say
- have difficulty recounting a story in the correct order of events
- have trouble remembering numbers
- have trouble telling time
- often misunderstand what is said
- request that information be repeated
- show a reluctance to talk

- use imprecise words or phrases

- use only a few descriptive words

Similar problems may be seen at school, so if your child's teacher mentions any of the following issues, it may be time to consider the possibility of dyslexia. In an academic setting, your child may:

- do poorly in noisy situations

- exhibit unexplained behavioral problems

- forget the question when called upon in class

- have difficulty reading or spelling

- have difficulty with math

- have problems remembering or following oral instructions

- have problems with phonics

- seem to daydream in class

- struggle with ambiguous language, idioms, or homonyms

- substitute the right answer with a different answer

While the symptoms described above could be considered the classic characteristics of dyslexia, there are a number of other clues that may point this condition. Your child may have difficulty:

- avoiding running into objects

- catching or throwing a ball

- knowing right from left

- organizing living spaces

- picking up small objects

- prioritizing tasks

- understanding directional signs

- walking fluidly

Some of these symptoms may be signs of certain other complex conditions that have been associated with dyslexia, including ADHD and dyscalculia. Considering the possibility of these interconnected issues can help paint a more detailed picture of your child's situation, which may lead to better solutions.

ASSOCIATED CONDITIONS

Unfortunately, when a child has dyslexia—or what I call dyslexia spectrum syndrome—there are frequently more conditions at play. Problems such as dyscalculia, dysgraphia, dyspraxia, and ADHD often go hand in hand with dyslexia. Recognizing that additional issues may be affecting your child is important. It is also important to note that, as with dyslexia, many of these problems can be overcome with the proper intervention.

Dyscalculia

The word *dyscalculia* is derived from the Greek term *dys*, which means "difficult," and the Latin term *calculare*, which means "to count." In other words, people with dyscalculia have trouble with math. As with dyslexia, the symptoms of this condition can vary from person to person and may include:

- absentmindedness
- difficulty grasping concepts of formal music education, such as sight-reading musical notation and learning fingering on an instrument
- difficulty visualizing mechanical processes
- difficulty with abstract concepts like time and direction
- poor name and face retrieval
- problems with money, credit, financial planning, budgeting, and balancing a checkbook, as well as fear of money and cash transactions
- trouble following rules in sports and keeping score of games

- trouble grasping and remembering math concepts, rules, formulas, sequences, and basic addition, subtraction, multiplication, and division

- trouble recalling schedules and sequences of past or future events

Although dyscalculia causes issues with math and numbers, a person with this condition may have normal or even accelerated verbal, reading, or writing skills, as well as poetic ability. Additionally, until a higher degree of math skill is needed, a person with dyscalculia will often do well in the sciences.

Dysgraphia

A person with dysgraphia has trouble with handwriting, which is usually distorted and illegible. Sometimes the letters in a word are different sizes. Often the spaces between words are missing. Words may be written in a combination of uppercase and lowercase letters, with the uppercase letters appearing in the middle of words. Lowercase letters in a word may be as large as the uppercase ones. A lowercase letter "p" or "g" may be completely above the line. A person with dysgraphia may also write backwards (from right to left) or upside down. Additionally, half of the words in a sentence may be written in cursive, while the other half is printed.

Along with handwriting problems, a person with dysgraphia may have trouble spelling, putting thoughts on paper, drawing, copying, or using maps and diagrams. While writing, other clues to disgraphia may be evident, including:

- keeping a tight grip on the pen or pencil and holding it very close to the paper

- leaving out words in sentences

- omitting the ends of words

- saying aloud the word that is being written

- spelling the same word in a number of different ways

- taking a long time to write

Some physicians recommend that children with dysgraphia use computers to avoid having to write. While this may seem like a good idea, it isn't. Children who learn to write via the computer will miss vital neurological steps that help not only their handwriting but also their reading skills and physical coordination.

Dyspraxia and Sensory Processing Disorder

Dyspraxia is considered a chronic neurological disorder that affects the motor skills involved in tasks such as combing hair, gripping small objects, and coordinating the facial muscle movements needed to pronounce words. Other symptoms include:

- difficulty listening

- problems processing information

- weaknesses in comprehension

Unfortunately, many children who have this condition also suffer from a sensory integration issue known as Sensory Processing Disorder (SPD).

SPD is a neurological disorder that disrupts the brain's ability to process information received through the senses of touch, sight, hearing, smell, and taste. SPD also affects the body's vestibular system, which helps control balance, and its proprioceptive system, which deals with the unconscious movement of muscles, joints, ligaments, and tendons.

Most people with dyspraxia and SPD display delays in speech, language, and motor skills. They are typically overly sensitive to touch, noise, and scents, and may have difficulty staying focused. They are frequently impulsive and often on the go.

Attention Deficit-Hyperactivity Disorder

In approximately 25 percent of cases, dyslexic children also suffer from Attention Deficit-Hyperactivity Disorder, or ADHD (formerly known as Attention Deficit Disorder, or ADD). ADHD interferes with learning and behavioral control in childhood and compromises function in multiple areas throughout life. It can lead to significant educational, occupational, and family dysfunctions, and can be a contributor to a variety of health, social, and economic problems.

ADHD has three main characteristics: inattention, hyperactivity, and impulsivity. Symptoms of inattention include:

- appearing not to listen
- displaying an inability to stay organized
- getting bored before a task is completed
- having difficulty remembering instructions
- having trouble staying focused
- ignoring details
- making careless mistakes

Signs of hyperactivity are evident when a child:

- constantly fidgets and squirms
- has difficulty playing quietly or relaxing
- talks excessively

Finally, impulsivity can be seen when a child:

- cannot wait for a turn while playing a game
- frequently blurts out answers in class without waiting to be called on or even hearing the questions entirely
- guesses the answer to a problem rather than taking the time to solve it
- often interrupts others, intrudes on other people's conversations or games

ADHD is a medical diagnosis given to a child after an evaluation by a mental health professional or a medical doctor. Teachers are often the first one to validate a child's attention-related difficulties. Before school age, children may appear ADHD, but truly, there are so many possible reasons for the previously mentioned behaviors that it is often difficult to assess learning challenges until formal schooling begins. More and more, however, preschool teachers are suggesting children be tested for various issues, which

The Ritalin Riddle

The "quick fix" treatment for many symptoms of ADHD is a methylphenidate drug called Ritalin. Because Ritalin and Ritalin-type drugs work by increasing the activity of the central nervous system (CNS), children can often focus and calm down immediately after taking the prescription. In the beginning, this change may seem like a miracle. Over time, however, the drug's effectiveness often decreases while its side effects increase.

Ritalin comes with some serious downsides that you may not know about. In 2009, Dr. Gerald Hüther, head of the Department of Fundamental Neurobiological Research at the psychiatric clinic of Germany's Göttingen University, used brain scans to show that taking Ritalin actually inhibits or shuts down the prefrontal cortex—the primary part of the modern brain that is used in decision making.[1] According to the research of neuroscientist Jaak Panksepp, Ritalin actually depresses the play centers of the brain. In other words, Ritalin robs children of their playfulness and resourcefulness! Additionally, Ritalin is also known to mute the care and bonding centers in the brain.[2] Long-term use of Ritalin-type drugs is rarely recommended, partly because of the severity of their side effects.

Unfortunately, many children who come to see me are already taking a Ritalin-type drug, an antidepressant, and a sleep medication. Many parents, however, would prefer natural alternatives for their children. I applaud this forward-thinking approach. It is not an easy way, though. It means investing time and effort in your child on a daily basis over a period of months or years. Of course, I'm not saying there is never a time to use Ritalin, but it is rarely my first choice.

is not a bad idea. The earlier a child can get help, the better. The school system often suggests waiting to test for dyslexia, but a parent can request it. Please, for your child's sake, know your rights as a parent as well as your child's rights.

PSYCHOLOGICAL AND EMOTIONAL ISSUES

By the time Sandra was twelve, if a teacher asked her to read aloud in class, her response was, "Just give me an F." She added, "Somehow I figured out I had a choice. I didn't have to read aloud. I'd rather take the 'F' any day than read aloud." Needless to say, Sandra did not go on to college. As was true in Sandra's case, "saving face," or somehow trying to salvage her honor and dignity in the moment, is a common strategy for children who feel unable to win the spelling bee or earn a college scholarship. They might even earn a reputation for being smart-mouthed or "clever."

When children aren't doing well in school or aren't happy, parents need to play detective and find the underlying cause of the problem. In a school setting, children with dyslexia tend to be frustrated and embarrassed. Feeling different is an awful badge to wear. The frustration a dyslexic feels can manifest itself psychologically and emotionally. Issues such as anger, depression, anxiety, and lack of confidence are tell-tale signs of dyslexia. It might be easier to brush off these behavioral problems and think that your child will outgrow them, but these symptoms should not be taken lightly or ignored. When a child is angry or fearful, learning becomes almost impossible.

Withdrawal

Wanting to be alone and pulling away from others are common ways in which children exhibit the frustrations of dyslexia. I have worked with many dyslexic kids who have told me that they sit by themselves during lunch and don't join in with others at recess—not because they really want to be alone, but because they don't think the other kids want to be with them. Children may withdraw voluntarily to avoid the disappointment of not being chosen for activities such as play dates or sports teams. Avoidance and withdrawal behavior may indicate a problem, but remember that wanting to spend some time alone may be perfectly fine and typical for a child. It is important to step back and consider the entire child before suspecting dyslexia.

Situational Depression

Unlike depression caused by a chemical imbalance, situational depression is the result of particular circumstances. Unfortunately, the circumstances brought about by dyslexia can easily lead to depression. Generally speaking, children who are depressed don't smile much. They avoid eye contact and tend to keep to themselves. They are frequently tired and slow in their motions. They feel stifled, as if boxed into a hopeless situation.

It is easy to dismiss this quietness. It is easy to say, "They'll get over it," or "They'll figure it out eventually." Sometimes kids simply shut down, and it is hard to get any information out of them. This does not mean you should turn the other way—quite the contrary. Ignoring the problem or going into denial can lead to disaster for your child and your family.

Anger and Aggression

When a child is embarrassed or frustrated in the classroom, these feelings can seem too strong to contain and lead to an eruption of anger. This explosion could be mild and fleeting, or intense and long lasting—sometimes to the point of violence. It may be released in the direction of teachers or classmates. Other times, this anger may be bottled and released at family members in the home. For example, one mother I met told me that her eleven-year-old dyslexic daughter would "hold it together" in school, only to take out her frustrations on her brother at home, taunting him mercilessly. This mother understood her daughter's anger, but was still at her wits' end.

Self-Destructive Behavior

When anger is turned inward, children may take to injuring themselves with sharp objects, sometimes called "cutting." Cutting is a form of self-mutilation done primarily by teenagers. It sounds like an extreme way of calling for attention or relieving emotional pain, but it is becoming more and more common. When children display such behavior, especially when it is prolonged, parents may be referred to someone in the medical field. Medications may be prescribed, such as antidepressants or anti-anxiety drugs. These medications, however, come with very serious possible side effects. It is important to note that there are a number of natural alternatives that may work just as well, and without the side effects.

Drug and Alcohol Use

Is it any wonder that a child who is suffering would want to numb the emotional and psychological pain of life? Many teens tell me that the only time they feel normal is when they are drunk or on drugs such as marijuana. Even Ritalin has become a street drug, bought and sold in schoolyards and snorted. Because Ritalin is very similar to cocaine in its chemical structure, the euphoria it produces can command a considerable price. Feeling empty or incapable can lead a child to a high-risk life. It is important to listen to what your child is telling you, whether in words or by actions.

Fear and Anxiety

A 2010 Roper Poll revealed that 80 percent of Americans equate dyslexia with mental retardation. Astonishing and appalling, but true. The fact that dyslexics are judged so harshly because they stumble over words, mispronounce them, or just plain guess at them is not fair. These judgments do not give an accurate view of the person as a whole, but they happen nevertheless. Fear may be evident in a dyslexic child who, in an effort to avoid being ridiculed for saying the wrong answer, does not speak up. This fear can become chronic anxiety, keeping a child awake at night and disrupting natural body rhythms. In time, anxiety can cause ulcers and digestive problems. Nervousness can lead to a depressed immune system, which increases the likelihood of catching viruses and missing school. If left unchecked, fear and apprehension can lead to long-term health issues and motivational problems.

Role Playing

In an effort to compensate for their frustration and maintain a sense of self, a dyslexic child will often take on a "role." The class clown, the bully, the mischief-maker, and the smart-aleck are just some of the personality types that may arise due to dyslexia. Sometimes playing a role can bring forth a strong suit in a dyslexic child that may serve him well in later life. Other times, playing a role can hold him back.

A DIFFERENCE, NOT A DISEASE

Dyslexia is not a disease, nor is it a mental or physical handicap. A dyslexic person simply has a mind that has chosen a different, less conventional way of learning and of viewing the world. Very often, in fact, this mind is gifted and displays amazing strengths in other areas. Sometimes these talents are apparent early on in life, and sometimes it takes years for them to emerge. I have worked with numerous dyslexic children who possessed a range of impressive strengths in many different areas. I've known children who had a natural eye for design and went on to enjoy satisfying careers as graphic artists, interior decorators, and fashion designers. I have had other patients who, despite having

The Dyslexia Label

Sometimes being labeled dyslexic brings a sigh of relief from knowing that the mystery of your situation has been solved. Realizing that you are not the only person dealing with this particular condition can be very comforting. Other times, the label of dyslexia is a ready-made excuse to avoid tackling the problem. It's too easy to think or say, "Oh, I can't do that. I'm dyslexic."

You become a victim of your circumstances, of your label. *You become the label.* What you believe about yourself—your own labeling—can have a profound effect on your life's direction.

When it comes to the label of dyslexia, your thoughts play a large role in overcoming this issue. Positive thoughts can lead to a positive change, while negative thoughts can generate a negative outcome. Unfortunately, conventional science and medicine have too many people convinced that dyslexics are victims, and that dyslexia is irreversible. These outdated beliefs are enough to make dyslexics feel hopeless, robbed of any power and potential.

But what if you had up-to-date information that proves that the brain can be changed? Would a diagnosis of dyslexia seem like such a dead end? Of course not. The truth is that being labeled dyslexic is not the problem; the real problem is the system at large that surrounds dyslexia. Although it is not yet widely known, there is scientifically validated research that shows that the brain can be rewired and dyslexia potentially reversed. In other words, old thoughts about dyslexia need to be thrown out, so that the negativity of labeling finally disappears.

dyslexia, were extremely business-savvy, and their clear entrepreneurial vision led them to become successful owners of their own companies. According to a Cass Business School study, 35 percent of entrepreneurs in the United States identify themselves as dyslexic.[3]

TALENTED (AND DYSLEXIC)

Although people with dyslexia may have problems with words and reading, they are often gifted in other areas. The following list of dyslexic individuals—which includes artists, architects, entertainers, physicians, political leaders, scientists, entrepreneurs, and athletes—proves that dyslexia need not stand in the way of success.

Ansel Adams	Patrick Dempsey	Jay Leno
Muhammad Ali	Walt Disney	Charles Lindbergh
Ludwig van Beethoven	Thomas Edison	Jack Nicholson
Orlando Bloom	Albert Einstein	George Patton
Richard Branson	F. Scott Fitzgerald	Pablo Picasso
Erin Brockovich	Harrison Ford	Nelson Rockefeller
George Burns	Henry Ford	Nolan Ryan
Jim Carrey	Bill Gates	Charles Schwab
Lewis Carroll	Danny Glover	Will Smith
Enrico Caruso	Whoopi Goldberg	Steven Spielberg
Cher	Woody Harrelson	Gwen Stefani
Agatha Christie	Tommy Hilfiger	Quentin Tarantino
Winston Churchill	Dustin Hoffman	Ted Turner
George Clooney	Bruce Jenner	Vince Vaughn
Anderson Cooper	Magic Johnson	Andy Warhol
Tom Cruise	John F. Kennedy	Robin Williams
Leonardo da Vinci	Keira Knightley	Henry Winkler
	John Lennon	

One of the most important responsibilities of parents is to help bring out the strengths of their children. When parents address a child's gifts as well as struggles, when they see their children as capable, they will help foster these strengths. I promise you, the time and effort put forth now will pay enormous dividends.

CONCLUSION

Dyslexia is a more complex and complicated condition than most people realize. To address only one aspect of the issue without standing back and looking at the entire picture may lead to more confusion and disappointment. Recognizing the numerous signs of dyslexia can help you understand that your child is not lacking in intelligence or capability. If you suspect dyslexia, you can take comfort in the fact that this learning issue is one of difference, not disability. Armed with the knowledge that dyslexia is often associated with other difficult conditions such as ADHD and Sensory Processing Disorder, you may begin to see your child in a completely new light—and this illumination can lead to positive change.

Shedding light on dyslexia and realizing that it can be overcome are the best ways to reverse or avoid the psychological and emotional problems that plague children with this condition. As mentioned earlier, the first step in successfully treating dyslexia comes by recognizing that the condition is more than just a reading problem. The second step comes by understanding that dyslexia need not hold back any child from achieving success in life, and may not even be a permanent condition.

3.

The Divided Brain

The makeup of the brain determines the way in which a person learns. The central nervous system comprises the brain and spinal cord, and uses nerves, which are like roads or channels, to carry information to and from the brain. Many of the basic building blocks of the central nervous system are assembled while a child is still in the womb and during the first few years of life. One layer is constructed, and then the next is generated over top, and so on. When circumstances affect the growth or connectivity of certain building blocks, the assembly line forges on regardless, disrupting the proper timing of development and weakening neurological foundations. When one layer lacks strength, subsequent layers may be underdeveloped, overdeveloped, or lopsided. This cascade of events can throw the entire central nervous system out of whack, causing a lack of integration that leads to learning problems.

A child needs a properly maturing central nervous system in order to function optimally, with brain and body working together as a cohesive unit. Unfortunately, so much of this neurological wiring occurs without conscious control. You may not realize that a problem exists until your child starts school, and by then, many links between building blocks may have already formed improperly. Luckily, these issues can be corrected—the process simply takes a little more effort. It becomes necessary to understand the brain as divided into three major areas: the reptilian brain, the limbic system, and the neocortex. This concept is often overlooked in connection with dyslexia, but it is actually integral to reversing this type of condition.

THE TRIUNE BRAIN

During the 1970s, neuroscientist Paul D. MacLean of the National Institute of Mental Health proposed an evolutionary theory of the brain called the Triune Brain model. This model provides a useful way of looking at the process behind dyslexia and points to possible improvements that can be made in treatment. The Triune Brain theory suggests that humans come equipped with three brains—the reptilian brain, the limbic system, and the neocortex—each of which develops in sequence, and each of which has particular qualities and strengths.[1] When fully integrated, these three brains communicate with each other via the limbic system, or middle brain. When they cannot talk effectively to each other, the affected individual may seem slightly out of sync, temporarily or throughout life.

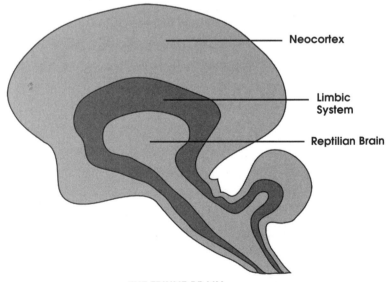

Neocortex

Limbic System

Reptilian Brain

THE TRIUNE BRAIN

The Reptilian Brain

Development of the reptilian brain, also called the primitive brain or the basic brain, begins in the womb and continues until approximately fifteen months after birth. The reptilian brain deals with basic safety issues, instinctual behaviors such as aggression, and the need to establish territory and survive. Until the survival and safety requirements of the reptilian brain are met, signals that enable higher brain function will not be communicated. When upper-level brain function fails, learning and behavioral problems may follow. In light of this fact, it is in the reptilian brain that many of the beginnings of dyslexia may lie.

The Limbic System

The limbic system, also called the paleomammalian brain or the emotional brain, is the next to develop. This system emerges at approximately fifteen months of age and continues to mature until a child is approximately five years old. It focuses on relationship issues, such as attachment, bonding, and nurturing. Emotion, motivation, and a sense of belonging to a family are all generated within the limbic system. As this brain grows, the individual learns how to relate to others and begins to explore emotions. Essentially, the limbic system is what makes a person a social being. These traits are crucial to an integrated central nervous system, and more important to learning than they may seem.

The Neocortex

The neocortex, also called the neomammalian brain or the thinking brain, is the last to evolve. Interestingly, it is the only type of brain that other members of the animal kingdom do not share. This modern brain gives humans the capacity for language, planning, and abstract thought. The development of these higher mental functions begins at approximately five years of age and lasts until the age of twenty-one and even beyond. The neocortex comprises two separate halves called the right and left hemispheres, each of which possesses distinct strengths. These hemispheres are connected by a bridge of neural fibers known as the corpus collosum.

FEAR AND LEARNING

Have you ever been caught off guard by a question and simply drew a blank, even though you actually knew the answer? Has someone badgered you for a response but you just couldn't think of the right one? The reason for these cognitive delays lies within the reptilian brain, which handles basic survival and safety issues. When a person is surprised, attacked, or ridiculed, this primitive brain generally reacts in one of three ways: fight, flee, or freeze. Given the right circumstances, the reptilian brain can shut down even the smartest individual. Childhood trauma, fear, insecurity, and overstimulation create precisely the conditions in which the reptilian brain takes over, inhibiting a child's ability to learn effectively.

When the reptilian brain is in charge, pathways to the higher brains are blocked, and thus the central nervous system cannot complete signals between each layer. Fear and uncertainty cause a child to retreat, defend a position, and react, rather than consider another point of view or feel a sense of emotional attachment. The fact is that at least 75 percent of all communication to the thinking part of the brain is cut off when a person is frightened. A child who does not feel safe will not try something new or risk the humiliation of getting an answer wrong. In a school setting, when children are frequently asked to do a task at which they are not adept, they often retract, become still and silent, breathe shallowly, and do not make a fuss. Conversely, if they feel backed against the wall, they may lash out and talk back to the teacher. Survival instincts are vital, of course, but we all lose when survival becomes the predominant operating system. Joseph Chilton Pearce, an expert in the field of birthing and child development, suggests that each person is faced with one major question throughout a lifetime: Must I defend, or can I grow and expand?[2]

In other words, until the reptilian brain is satisfied, any attempts to learn will be disrupted.

You've seen the reptilian brain in action, haven't you? It is behind the aggression, the smart-mouthed comments, the walking or running away in the middle of a challenging conversation, the sulking fits, and the deer-in-the-headlights looks. These behaviors are typical of kids who have been labeled learning disabled, but may be the signs of a reptilian brain that simply needs to be calmed and reassured. Unfortunately, when a child feels different or is not learning in the way that other kids are, a vicious circle may be created in which the individual is in a constant state of survival, always reacting in defense against further insult.

MOVEMENT AND LEARNING

The vestibular system is concerned with balance, orientation in time and space, and coordination of muscles. It develops at the same time as the reptilian brain and is responsible for connecting all the information taken in through the body's various senses. When the vestibular system is functioning properly, a child is able to explore the world fully and learn effectively. As an infant grows, physical movements map pathways throughout the central nervous system, which allow for proper integration of brain functions later on. This is why the reflexes that take hold during the first months of life are so important. They are vital to the building blocks of the brain, which must be created in correct sequence.

When children crawl, they are mimicking all four-legged creatures that turn towards sounds with their ears rather than their eyes. Crawling exercises the vestibular system, promoting balance, hearing, and a proper sense of gravity. Moreover, when children reach for and touch objects, they become aware of space and distance. When children begin to sit or stand, they also begin to look around more, thus orienting themselves through the eyes. These actions help note auditory and visual input and create connections in the brain, strengthening coordination.

Every time a baby moves, the action wakes up parts of the brain and sends out myelin to make future movements faster and easier. Myelin—a white layer of insulation around nerve cells—builds up with use and speeds transmission of impulses across

Teresa's Story

Teresa was about nine years old when her parents brought her to me for a consultation. She was wearing glasses and her hair was in pigtails. One of the first things I had Teresa do was walk up and down the hallway a few times. I had her parents stand behind me so they could watch as I pointed out how her right arm swung more than her left, and how her right leg seemed to do more of the walking while the left trailed along. I then asked Teresa to stand facing the door while her parents and I stood behind her, this time observing her posture. One shoulder was higher than the other, making her entire body seem uneven. The asymmetry of her posture and gait suggested some degree of neurological incongruence. When I asked Teresa's mother about her daughter's infant years, she proudly explained, "Teresa only crawled for one week. She started walking almost immediately and never wanted to crawl after that." The puzzle pieces began to fit.

When a child crawls, the eyes watch the hand moving from left to right repeatedly, just as the eyes move when reading. But Teresa's eyes had experienced only one week of moving from left to right and back again instead of several months. Early walking often makes parents feel that their child is gifted, but this accomplishment may come with a price. Had she crawled longer, Teresa may have acquired stronger physical coordination and better posture. The improved symmetry of her body may have also resulted in fewer learning problems.

Thankfully, neural circuitry can change. After her therapy sessions, in which certain exercises were performed to establish proper connections within her body, new information began to be easily taken in and relayed throughout her brain and nervous system. Her improved physicality even helped her to be picked first for the school soccer team!

cells. So cognitive functions (thought) and motor functions (movement) are actually part of the same system, even though they have historically been viewed as separate. It could be said that thinking, a higher brain function, is fueled by movement. Unfortunately, many experts in the field of dyslexia downplay the role of the body in the learning process. In order for the brain and body to function smoothly, however, the issue of dyslexia needs to be addressed at these beginning stages, not by dealing merely with the symptom of reading problems.

ATTACHMENT AND LEARNING

Sitting above the reptilian brain but below the neocortex, the limbic system has relay stations that allow communication between all three brains. It plays an important role in a healthy immune system as well as neural integration and learning. A properly functioning limbic system allows emotions to come and go, preventing a person from getting stuck in any one emotion, such as anger or fear. (The reptilian brain, of course, has to be well controlled and integrated in order for the limbic system to allow these emotions to flow through appropriately.) It encourages bonding and attachment with the help of a chemical in the brain known as oxytocin. Even the simple gesture of petting a dog will release oxytocin and promote a sense of caring. In fact, kids in alternative home situations such as juvenile detention centers are sometimes given dogs or horses to care for in an effort to strengthen emotional bonding.

A properly nurtured limbic system boosts self-esteem and motivates children to learn. When a child has a good sense of self and a peaceful reptilian brain, motivation bubbles up from within naturally. Without these factors, a child may seem detached, aimless, or just plain lost. When the limbic brain is not functioning well, chaos can break out. Emotions can get out of control, evidenced by hurt feelings, depression, and even suicidal thoughts. A weak limbic system causes all reason and logic to go out the window and severely hampers learning.

CREATIVITY AND LEARNING

One of the most important facts to know about the neocortex is that its two hemispheres develop at different times. The right hemisphere begins to blossom around the age of three or four. Creativity and imagination explode during this time, and life is fun. By the age of seven or eight, the left hemisphere—with its more logical, linear, and sequential thinking—starts to play a significant role. Neurologically and developmentally, this is the ideal time to start reading (which is exactly what happens in Denmark, but not in many other countries). Before the age of eight, the level of development of the neocortex suggests that kids should be out-

Angela's Story

The first time fifteen-year-old Angela appeared in my office, she had a certain faraway look in her eye that concerned me. In addition to her dyslexia, Angela's examination revealed that she saw herself in a distorted, negative way. Knowing that self-destructive tendencies often accompany neurological problems of the visual and vestibular systems, I decided to give Angela an assignment. "Between now and next time I see you, I want you to write down all the things you would like to see different in your life," I said.

At Angela's next appointment, she produced a two-page list of all the things she didn't like about herself and wished could be different. Two whole pages! I read them, and then I looked her softly but directly and said, "Now tell me how you've considered suicide." Without missing a beat, she started telling me the various methods she had already contemplated. Throughout therapy, I was able to address the structural and neurological imbalances that were contributing to her negative attitude. Her dyslexia improved and so did her state of mind.

Today, Angela is very much alive and doing well. Having successfully completed both high school and college, she now enjoys a career at a public relations and marketing firm.

side playing and interacting with their environment, exercising their field of vision from near to far and back again, all of which readies the body for reading and learning. Asking a child to focus for long periods on a book (or a handheld videogame) before the left hemisphere is ready is not developmentally correct.

In addition to the right and left hemispheres, there are several other parts of the neocortex worthy of mention. The prefrontal cortex and frontal lobes deal with associative thinking (sorting out and synthesizing information), executive function (planning and decision making), and working memory (keeping information available for comprehension and processing). As mentioned earlier, the corpus callosum—the bridge between the two hemispheres—is another crucial element of the neocortex, as it allows information to flow from one side to the other.

With different parts responsible for so many higher functions, the neocortex has often been called a crown of jewels. When these parts are connected and integrated with the rest of the brain, the neocortex allows the individual to explore new vistas and advance in both the arts and sciences. When the neocortex lacks integration or its right and left sides are out of sync, it can easily turn into a crown of thorns, leading to dyslexia and other learning conditions.

Left-Brain Bias

Developmental psychologist Howard Gardner states that people can be smart in different ways. In the United States, however, most people still think being smart means using the logical left brain, and view the strengths of the right side as inferior. Just watch which part of the school budget is cut when money is tight. It's not left-brain subjects like math and science. It's typically music and art, for which the right brain is responsible. Even the teachers of math and science enjoy a higher status than music and art teachers within most schools.

Although the traditional educational system favors left-brain learning styles, it would behoove us all to note that the right brain develops before the left brain. This little fact is important to the process of learning. Whenever a person attempts to learn something new, it is best to address the information according to the same sequence in which the brain developed. In most school systems, learning is often approached in a backwards manner, focusing on the left brain first. This method makes the practice more difficult than necessary. I believe that starting the learning process with the left brain is like swimming upstream against the current. It is possible to do, but it is so much harder than swimming with the current.

Thankfully, in recent years, the talents of the right brain are gaining respect. This change can be seen especially in Master of Business Administration (MBA) programs, which have been emphasizing marketing and creativity more and more. The fact is that the working world is starting to realize that it needs people who are talented in both hemispheres of the neocortex. It is beginning to embrace a whole-brain approach, so to speak. The upside of this new attitude in business is that it may spur an effort to revamp the antiquated educational system and, in doing so, get people learning in the right way.

The Problem with Passive Learning

Many of my colleagues have embraced the idea of banning TV before the age of eight so that the creative skills of the right brain have a chance to bloom. The right brain starts to develop by the age of two and is in its prime from the age of four to seven. During this period, children learn best by moving and interacting with other children as well as their environment. Television is passive, which means the information is spoon-fed to the child and can remain unintegrated forever. Have you ever noticed kids parroting the words from television but not really having a clue what they mean?

CONCLUSION

Dyslexia and most other learning challenges have a neurological basis. Proper integration of the various neurological areas is crucial to a child's ability to learn. One layer of the brain needs to be complete and fully functioning for the next part to become strong and stable, and for communication within the entire central nervous system to become cohesive and clear. Early in life, physical movement promotes important visual and auditory mapping within the brain. In addition, physical movement "greases" the brain so that it can work faster and more efficiently. Natural neural development helps ensure proper overall balance. If a stage is missed or the timing of development is slightly off, problems may arise in the future. Thankfully, it is possible to retrain and update the brain, but therapy must address each part of this organ according to the sequence in which it evolved. This is why the problem of dyslexia cannot be reversed through treatment that focuses only on the highest layer of the brain.

Therapies that attempt to treat dyslexia by looking only at its superficial symptoms, such as reading difficulties, are insufficient and often create more frustration for all parties involved. By not delving deep enough into the issue, key causes of dyslexia are ignored or glossed over. These causes may actually lie beneath the higher-functioning neocortex, in the reptilian brain or limbic system. By avoiding deeper issues, the channels of communication between the reptilian brain, limbic system, and neocortex continue to malfunction, preventing normal emotional function and blocking access to the areas of the brain necessary to process new information. When treatment focuses solely on the task of reading, it goes about solving the problem backwards, forgetting that the normal development of the neocortex begins with the creative, which is fueled by play and motion, and then proceeds to the logical.

By understanding the natural evolution and functions of the three different brains, dyslexia can be reversed in almost all cases. Once the importance of proper overall brain integration is realized and incorporated into therapy, dyslexia may become nothing more than a temporary inconvenience.

4.

Rewiring the Brain

For years, scientists viewed the brain as an unchangeable organ. According to popular thought, the brain was considered set, or "hardwired," after a small window of rapid development during early childhood and a slower period of growth during adolescence, with only deterioration to follow with age. Naturally, a problem such as dyslexia was also considered unchangeable. Most doctors assumed no possibility of adjusting the way the brain works, focusing instead on workarounds to help dyslexics compensate. The notion of reversing dyslexia was out of the question. Recently, however, research has revealed evidence that contradicts this long-held view. Remarkable discoveries in neuroscience have shed light on the amazing roles that neuroplasticity and epigenetics play in brain function.

Neuroplasticity deals with the ability of the brain to change its structure in response to experience, while the science of epigenetics shows how external stimuli can turn genes on or off. Together these fields are creating a completely new way for both professionals and parents to view dyslexia. It is no longer wishful thinking to hope that dyslexia is reversible; in most cases, it is very possible. Just as the world was proven not to be flat after all, new research is demonstrating that the makeup of the brain is not fixed. A dyslexic brain can change and rewire itself. While traditional treatment of dyslexia may not acknowledge this fact, many modern alternative therapies attempt to repair every layer of brain development, starting from the ground up. They focus on reversing the issue instead of simply teaching dyslexic patients techniques to compensate for their learning difference. This represents an important change in the way this condition is perceived, and one that will continue to gain traction in the scientific community as informed patients become advocates of these new treatment methods.

NEUROPLASTICITY

Scientific thought has been dominated by the belief that the brain has completed its development once a person reaches adulthood, and that the only way this organ changes after this point is for the worse, due to aging, disease, or physical trauma. According to this perspective, if a brain cell has been damaged or destroyed, there is little hope of neural repair or regrowth. In short, if you have been born with cognitive limitations, you will be stuck with these issues for the rest of your life. (Is it any wonder that most educators genuinely see dyslexia as a permanent and irreversible condition?) The truth, however, is that the brain is plastic—constantly learning, changing, and growing (or shrinking). Neuroplasticity refers to the idea that the brain can repair or create new neural pathways in response to external experience, essentially remapping itself to restore proper functionality.

Barbara Arrowsmith Young is a pioneer in the use of neuroplasticity to treat learning disorders. Born in the 1950s, she grew up severely dyslexic but also very smart. Her brain was asymmetrical, which means it did not develop evenly on both sides or even within each of its halves. While this asymmetry seemed to give her an almost perfect memory when it came to auditory and visual stimuli, it also created confusion, chaos, and uneven learning. Like many children with learning problems, she doubted her intelligence and even wondered if she might be crazy. At that time, unfortunately, learning disabilities were not labeled and there were no teachers equipped to deal with such matters. Despite her challenges, Barbara did not give up on her education. Like many successful dyslexics, she became tenacious and tried to learn in any way she could, pushing herself all the way to graduate school.

In her mid-twenties, Barbara came across published research that showed how the brains of rats were reshaped by exposure to certain external stimuli. This information contradicted the idea that the brain was a static and unchangeable organ, and was the first inkling of neuroplasticity. Barbara loved the idea that the brain could actually change and not merely compensate, and began designing neurological exercises to retrain her brain. Slowly but surely, her brain began to function normally. She soon used her knowledge to help other children with learning disorders, discerning the specific areas where dyslexic children have difficulty, developing exercises to recharge and strengthen those weak areas, and teaching dyslexic brains to process information in new ways. Eventually, she started a school for children with learning problems. Today there are thirty-five schools in North America that utilize her approach. While Barbara has been using her skills to reverse dyslexia for a long time, the established scientific community is only now beginning to embrace the notion of neuroplasticity and all that it entails.

EPIGENETICS

Another branch of scientific study that has been gaining ground in recent years, epigenetics has the potential to revolutionize medicine and positively affect the treatment of learning disorders. Focused on the role of genes and heredity, epigenetics purports that genes may be turned on or off in reaction to environmental factors.

With the help of the deoxyribonucleic acid (DNA) and ribonucleic acid (RNA) contained within, genes control both the external appearance and internal function of every living thing. It was long believed that the expression of RNA and DNA could only work in one direction. This idea has now been proven wrong. Genetic expression is not completely out of a person's control after all. According to scientists such as cell biologist Dr. Bruce Lipton, the DNA in genes is controlled by signals outside the cell. Experience and environment influence genes and can affect whether or not particular genes are activated.

This is a very important idea when it comes to learning problems such as dyslexia. Those people who have a genetic predisposition for this disorder understandably think there is nothing that can be done if dyslexia rears its head. Epigenetics suggests that this belief may be untrue. We are not completely controlled by our genes, and the fact that you may have dyslexia does not

A Brain Reorganized

Pedro Bach-y-Rita, a poet and scholar, suffered a disabling stroke at the age of sixty-five. It paralyzed his face and half of his body, leaving him unable to speak. His family was told there was no hope of recovery and that Pedro should be institutionalized. One of his sons ignored this advice, disregarded conventional medical wisdom, and decided to retrain his father's brain. They began by crawling together for months, and then played marbles and other floor games to recover Pedro's fine motor skills. At the age of sixty-eight, Pedro was able to teach college again. He remarried, worked, hiked, and traveled for another seven years. He eventually died of a heart attack while mountain climbing in Bogota, Columbia.

After his death, the autopsy revealed that 97 percent of the nerves that run from the brain to the spine had been destroyed by the stroke years earlier. Amazingly, the therapy Pedro underwent with his son had reorganized his brain function enough for him to resume college-level teaching using only 3 percent of this organ.

If a brain at sixty-five could be simulated and reorganized at only 3-percent capacity, think of the possibilities the right therapy might provide a child with a learning disability.

mean it cannot be reversed by turning certain genes on or off. As stated by Dr. Lipton, "We can be totally healthy. We can rewrite the genes to make them normal."[1] The idea that genes can be manipulated and influenced means that dyslexics may be able to adjust their learning processes without using workarounds or pharmaceuticals.

THE DOWNSIDE TO NEUROPLASTICITY

Are you concerned about the amount of time your child spends playing video games or sitting in front of the computer? Neuroplasticity reveals a major downside to the ways in which children spend most of their free time these days. In the same way that the plasticity of the brain can lead to beneficial changes, it can also result in harmful ones. As renowned psychiatrist Dr. Norman Doidge states, "Electronic media are extensions of our nervous systems: the telegraph, radio, and telephone extend the range of the human ear, the television camera extends the eye and sight, the computer extends the processing capacities of our central nervous system."[2] Media as we know it may not only stimulate the senses but also alter them in ways you may not realize or desire. When you engage with computers and other electronic gadgets for hours on end, certain areas of your brain are being overexercised to the detriment of others.

Another area of concern with electronic devices such as video games, television, and computers involves the processing speed of the brain versus that of these machines. When a person interacts with these media, things happen at a much faster pace than in real life. A slew of information enters the brain quickly and passively, leading to a lack of proper integration. People sometimes feel drained after watching television because the practice does not allow enough time for the rapid images to be processed effectively. Unfortunately, people often enjoy the feeling these fast-paced scenes produce and begin to acquire a need for this lightening pace. Before long, they find slower actions boring. As Doidge points out, "the cost is that such activities as reading, complex conversation, and listening to lectures become more difficult."[3] Make no mistake; neuroplasticity offers considerable benefits to the nervous system. It has freed people from the notion of being stuck by their previous limitations. It is, however, a two-way street. We need to be aware that overexposure to electronic media can negatively affect a person's ability to learn complex ideas and interact with others. A favorite saying in the field of neuroplasticity is, "Neurons that fire together, wire together." This means that whenever you do an action over and over again, you make certain neural connections stronger and increase the speed with which you can learn similar tasks. The downside of this plasticity is that the old adage "use it or lose it" is also true, meaning important connections can decay or atrophy without use.

A Child Made Whole Again

Brandi Bryce was five years old when she started having seizures. Her behavior changed, and gradually she no longer sang, danced, or even played with other children. By age six, her family discovered that Brandi had a rare disease known as Rasmussen's encephalitis, and that the right side of her brain would have to be removed. Brandi's doctors told her parents that she would no longer be capable of doing activities typically associated with the right side of the brain, including abstract thought and anything artistic or creative.

Brandi's family did not accept this prognosis. They all pitched in to stimulate her brain in a myriad of ways over time. Eventually, her left brain not only performed the usual left-brain functions, but also functioned as her right brain, allowing her to draw, paint, and dance again. Amazingly, Brandi ended up graduating high school and college with high honors, proving that a child's brain has a miraculous ability to adapt and regain functions lost.

NEW THERAPIES FOR DYSLEXIA

Yale University medical professor Dr. Sally Shaywitz conducted a twenty-year study of dyslexia using sophisticated functional magnetic resonance imaging (fMRI), which measures brain activity by tracking changes in blood flow. She found that dyslexic readers used different parts of the brain than non-dyslexic readers used. When a non-dyslexic person read, the back, side, and front of the brain showed activity; when a dyslexic person read, predominantly the front of the brain displayed activity. These findings were of interest, as the sides and back of the brain are known to discriminate sounds, words, and shapes, while the front of the brain sees individual words as whole units. Being a more modern section of the brain, the front brain is ideally triggered only after the parts of the brain that deal with sound patterns, which are older developmentally, have first processed written information. By focusing on whole-word recognition, the dyslexic brains studied by Dr. Shaywitz missed valuable data necessary for smooth reading.

In addition to fMRIs, other new ways of gathering images of the brain such as positive emission tomography (PET scan), single-photo emission tomography (SPECT scan), and quantitative electroencephalograms (QEEG) are providing precise details of brain function that can improve the medical establishment's understanding of dyslexia and lead to better treatment. There is now enough evidence, much of which has been obtained through research funded by large universities such as Yale and MIT, to assert confidently that the brain can be rewired. Even a few individual therapists, including neurofeedback specialist Jonathan Walker, have published findings that display before and after changes in the brain. Amazingly, in a study of twelve dyslexic children, brains affected by dyslexia were shown to look more like non-dyslexic brains after being treated by Dr. Walker.[4]

As previously noted, just because the dyslexic brain skips certain necessary sequences during the process of reading does not mean that dyslexia is a permanent condition. The brain is plastic, and very capable of readjusting itself to read smoothly. New therapies approach the issue from this perspective. Unfortunately, due to cost, many of these new treatments have not yet taken advantage of advanced brain-imaging equipment to prove differences in the brain pre- and post-therapy; but the proof is in the pudding, as they say. When a new therapy is able to replicate its results in many patients, as the following examples have done, it should be considered useful. Essentially, case results must speak for themselves until research funding becomes available in connection with some of these newer approaches.

While many treatments hold great promise, please remember that there are no quick fixes or magic bullets when it comes to this matter. Each dyslexic person is unique and much too complex to fit into any "cookie cutter," one-size-fits-all treatment plan. Always be suspicious of any therapy that promises to work 100 percent of the time. Moreover, the novelty of certain treatments may mean that they are not yet covered by insurance, so becoming educated on these new methods of treating dyslexia is tremendously important. Knowledge of the following therapies will empower you to make the best possible decisions in connection with your or your child's condition.

Neurofeedback

Biofeedback uses special equipment to sense certain physiological functions. This information is then "fed back" to the user in an effort to increase awareness of these functions and even allow the user to gain control over them. It has been utilized for many years to manipulate processes such as brainwaves, heart rate, and pain perception. There are reputable biofeedback training and degree programs within psychology and health sciences departments at numerous universities throughout the country. Hundreds of biofeedback studies have been done with comprehensive, meticulous documentation.

Neurofeedback is a type of biofeedback that uses quantitative electroencephalograms or functional magnetic resonance imaging to map the brain. These maps can show the before and after changes in the brain in connection with the treatment of dyslexia or other neurological conditions. Essentially, this therapy consists of electrical stimulation to various areas of the brain. After a course of treatment, therapists look at the brain map for positive changes in neural pathways.

Understandably, neurofeedback is a useful therapy for those patients whose symptoms include obvious neurological, physical, or sensory-motor issues. Unfortunately, despite many years of established biofeedback work, most health insurance companies still consider neurofeedback to be experimental and will not cover it.

Interactive Metronome (IM)

When the timing mechanism through which the brain detects and processes information is faulty, problems with reading, attention, memory, and coordination often follow. A recent treatment addition to the field of learning disorders, Interactive Metronome focuses on these timing issues in the brain. It is used in various kinds of therapeutic settings, including occupational therapy and chiropractic offices. The patient wears headphones and attempts to match rhythmic beats with repetitive motor actions in the hope that the brain's timing mechanism might recalibrate. Proponents of IM see this therapy as functional neuroplasticity in action. IM may be used to treat symptoms associated with dyslexia such as attention and concentration problems, motor planning and sequencing disruptions, and balance and gait issues.

Educational Kinesiology (Edu-K) and Brain Gym

Kinesiology is the study of human movement. Educational Kinesiology, or Edu-K, is based on the premise that certain physical movements can improve brain function. Brain Gym is a system of twenty-six specific movements that have been designed to optimize learning. Brain Gym therapy generally consists of small classes wherein exercises are taught to parents and teachers, who then work directly with children. These exercises can be incorporated in school settings or professional offices such as pediatric chiropractors and kinesiologists, often in addition to other treatments. These movements are especially useful after the underlying neurology of a dyslexic patient has been corrected through other methods. They help reinforce proper eye function, which helps with reading, and whole-body movement, which strengthens focus and concentration.

CranioSacral Therapy (CST)

Created in the early 1980s by Dr. John Upledger, CranioSacral Therapy finds its origins in the field of osteopathy, which focuses on treating the person as a whole and attempts to make use of the body's self-healing mechanisms. The correlate in the field of chiropractic is called Sacral Occipital Technique (SOT). CST is a one-on-one approach that involves light touch on various parts of the patient's body to balance the various fluids and rhythms of the physical system. Many occupational therapists, physical therapists, and massage therapists incorporate CST into their overall methods of treatment. It may improve sensory-motor issues and difficulties with focus.

Touch for Health

Applied kinesiology is a field of alternative medicine that tests muscle strength to diagnose illness. Just as Dr. John Upledger modified the practice of cranial osteopathy to create CranioSacral Therapy, John Thie adapted the principles of applied kinesiology to invent the Touch for Health system. Touch for Health uses touch, massage, and acupressure techniques, which can improve posture and balance, and reduce tension. In doing so, Touch for Health may alleviate both the physical and mental issues of a patient.

Touch for Health serves as the basis of hundreds of applied kinesiology-based classes around the world and has been used as part of the overall treatment of numerous health and learning disorders. It has the potential to address many layers of the dyslexia problem.

Books Neural Therapy (BNT)

A treatment I designed personally, Books Neural Therapy is a gentle hands-on neurological and structural repatterning therapy. BNT addresses the body-brain integration issues that often accompany learning and behavioral problems. Using various therapies and exercises to improve gross and fine motor skills, centering, and posture, it encourages the left and right hemispheres of the brain to communicate properly. It also helps reorganize the central nervous system by realigning the cranial bones, which may have been misaligned due to head trauma. Additionally, BNT evaluates eye muscle coordination and corrects it if necessary. Finally, one of the unique features of BNT is its attention to basic brain patterns, where deep survival issues are stored and hidden. As noted earlier, the core of many dyslexic issues is housed in the deepest layer of the brain. Clearing the patient of physical and emotional roadblocks frees up natural learning sequences in the brain, allowing it to process information effectively. BNT addresses sensory-motor difficulties, problems with visual and auditory processing, as well as focus issues. It is typically performed by a licensed healthcare professional, though a nonprofessional online version of BNT (The Dyslexia Reversal System) is also available (www.drphyllisbooks.com).

Primitive Reflex Therapy

In the womb and during the early months after birth, reflexes controlled by the lowest layer of the brain help a child survive as the central nervous system develops and matures. These involuntary reactions are spurred by such stimuli as touch, sound, temperature, and hunger, and may involve body movement, breathing, and perceptual or hormonal changes. As the higher layers of the brain begin to take conscious control of certain activities, these primitive reflexes become integrated into the central nervous system to allow for this control. When they are integrated out of sequence, they may disturb the optimal development of subsequent upper-level brain functions, which include behavior, learning, and fine motor skills.

Primitive Reflex Therapy uses a series of exercises to reset the sequence of reflex reactions within the layers of the brain, attempting to integrate them in the right way and reverse any associated learning difficulties. This therapy is incorporated into sessions by occupational or physical therapists, chiropractors, and kinesiologists.

Tomatis Method

Developed by French physician Dr. Alfred Tomatis, the Tomatis Method is based on the view that most learning disorders are caused by hearing problems. Pioneering the idea that you can't reproduce a sound you don't hear, Dr. Tomatis created this auditory technique to help patients with dyslexia strengthen their listening, language, and communication skills. He devised a sound program that includes wearing headphones to listen to particular sounds and music. Although this therapy is relatively new to the United States, there are Tomatis Centers in several metropolitan areas, and some home-based programs are also available.

Advanced Brain Technologies (ABT)

Advanced Brain Technologies is the brainchild of Alex Doman, whose grandfather, Glen Doman, co-created a therapy called the Doman-Delacato Method to help brain-injured children improve the quality of their lives during the 1950s. Like the Tomatis Method, ABT is an auditory program which has patients listen to music and nature sounds through headphones in an effort to tune up auditory processing and reorganize proper connections in the central nervous system. There are home-based versions of ABT, which are often overseen by educational or occupational therapists.

Lindamood-Bell

Conceived in 1986 by Patricia Lindamood and Nanci Bell, this method is another auditory therapy. Created to improve reading, spelling, comprehension, and language expression, this approach was designed with the understanding that some people with reading disabilities have unreliable auditory perceptions. Simply put, they do not hear the various individual sounds, or phonemes, that make up whole words. The resultant learning disorders are addressed by teaching patients alternate ways to perceive the many phonemes that make up all the words in the English language. This therapy is conducted in a one-on-one setting for a few days a week over the course of several months. Lindamood-Bell is available in the private sector and occasionally through the public school system.

Sensory Integration Therapy

Sensory Integration Dysfunction, also called Sensory Processing Disorder, is characterized by the inability to organize information taken in by the senses (taste, smell, hearing, sight, and touch) for use by the brain. This dysfunction can result in numerous conditions, including learning problems such as dyslexia. Sensory Integration Therapy is a body-based technique performed by occupational therapists to help the underdeveloped sensory and motor skills associated with this disorder. It employs physical exercises, auditory training, and sensory stimulation or inhibition techniques to improve the integration of information in the brain. This therapy is available in the private sector and often through the public school system.

Vision Therapy

Performed primarily by specially trained developmental optometrists, vision therapy is a one-on-one exercise-based therapy for the eyes and brain. Designed to improve eye focus, eye movement control, and coordination between the two eyes, this method is helpful to patients with such visual problems as lazy eye, crossed eyes, double vision, and convergence, and may benefit patients whose reading difficulties stem from disorders of the visual system. Vision therapy uses eye exercises, lenses, filters, and other instruments, and is tailored to the individual patient's needs.

Irlen Method

Scotopic Sensitivity Syndrome, also known as Irlen Syndrome, theorizes that certain reading problems are due to the brain reacting improperly to specific wavelengths of light. The eyes function normally, but due to a defect in the visual pathways to the brain, a timing error occurs in the processing of visual information. Images appear like double-exposed photographs. The location of objects in an image seem out of place, so the brain tries to reconstruct the picture, resulting in the appearance of items moving around within the image, the image being blurry, holes in visual information, or other similar issues. Understandably, this syndrome can lead to learning difficulties, sore eyes, mental exhaustion, headaches, and trouble with concentration.

Created by Helen Irlen, the Irlen Method uses colored lenses to help people with Scotopic Sensitivity Syndrome. A professional therapist trained in the Irlen Method helps the patient find the right lens color, which will filter out certain wavelengths of light and restore optimal visual processing. Words stand still and reading problems disappear. Additionally, some Irlen Method cases have shown that therapy may allow the brain to learn which wavelengths are problematic so that the visual pathways can begin to filter them out on their own over time.

Fast ForWord

Developed by renowned scientists that include Michael Merzenich and Bill Jenkins, this computer-based program is meant to help children recognize sounds better and strengthen reading skills. Games such as speech-sound drills, in which sounds are processed and slowed down to exaggerate their differences, are used to improve temporal processing and organize the sounds heard in language. This auditory treatment has also been used by older people who simply want to turn back the clock on their brains and revitalize the way they process information.

Neuro Emotional Technique (NET)

According to the Center for Disease Control (CDC), 85 percent of illnesses have an emotional component. Unfortunately, it is not uncommon for a child to experience a negative situation that affects learning. These learning difficulties may persist until the emotional block is resolved. Taking this notion into account, Neuro Emotional Technique is a therapy that treats the individual holistically, addressing not only the physical aspects of a problem, but the emotional ones as well. It includes treatment approaches from many fields, including traditional Chinese medicine, applied kinesiology, and chiropractic. In addition to dealing with psychological issues, therapists look for structural imbalances, toxins in the body, and nutritional deficiencies, all of which may play a role in learning disorders. NET is typically performed by both chiropractors and psychologists.

HeartMath

Doc Childre developed HeartMath to help people transform stress and negativity into manageable states of mind. According to HeartMath, the heart has an intelligence that powerfully affects mental and physical health. There are thousands of neurons in the heart, and the signals they send can change activity in the central nervous system for better or worse. For example, when the rhythms of the heart are balanced, stress hormones decrease and there is a positive effect on the immune system. The HeartMath Institute works with educators, individuals, businesses, and even soldiers. It involves the use of computers, games, and music to reduce stress. It also employs specific psychological techniques such as Freeze-Frame, which allows people to change their view of stress and alter the way in which they react to a perceived crisis. This therapy helps with clarity and focus, and may be a worthwhile addition to other dyslexia treatments.

Emotional Freedom Technique (EFT)

Like HeartMath and Neuro Emotional Technique, EFT is a therapy that focuses on clearing the individual of emotional stumbling blocks and negativity. Essentially, it seeks to alleviate negative emotions such as fear, which may play a role in certain disorders, including dyslexia. As explained earlier, fear can shut a person down, disabling the ability to learn effectively. EFT may lift this barrier of fear and serve as part of the successful overall treatment of many cases of dyslexia.

EFT uses "tapping" techniques, which target specific points on the body much in the same way that acupuncture does. This practice is said to neutralize negative emotions that may be interfering with clarity and learning. EFT can be taught to anyone, but

Fear of Change

Many times patients say to me, "Don't take away my dyslexia. I like thinking in different ways and I don't want to lose that ability." Once dyslexic individuals have figured out how to function in the world with their condition, they become afraid of how they might manage even the slightest changes to their routine. They worry about turning "normal." Often dyslexics are highly successful people who actually attribute their achievements to the differences in their brains, which allow them to function so differently than most people. To address this concern I ask, "What would it be like to work with your whole brain, not just parts of it?" The talents and strengths of a dyslexic mind will not disappear when this condition is reversed. Rather, these characteristics will be joined by other qualities of the brain that have been dormant. Reversing dyslexia is about chipping away the parts that are not serving the individual so that a complete set of talents can come forth. It is about giving a dyslexic person access to the brain as a whole.

is best performed with the help of a qualified psychologist familiar with this therapy, who may get to the root of the problem much more quickly than a nonprofessional.

DECIDING ON A TREATMENT

When it comes to the treatment of dyslexia, there are many available choices, though mainstream medicine may not acknowledge this fact. Many of the previously referenced therapies, however, are considered alternative, which means they fall outside traditional approaches and will likely not be covered by health insurance. Although these innovative techniques have proven helpful to numerous people, some of them may lack the scientific data required to gain mainstream acceptance. Of course, as with any new treatment, it is always important to be wary of charlatans, who will say anything to get you to buy their products. So how can you judge what is unproven by traditional methods yet still may be a wise choice for you or your child? The best route to take is to speak to patients who have participated in the program you are considering. Usually, therapists will be able to provide you with a few names of people who have consented to having potential clients contact them directly. Once you have access to these patients, ask them any questions you may have, but be sure to inquire about the long-term results of the treatment being considered.

Treatment Integration

After working with dyslexic and other learning-challenged children and adults over the past twenty-five years, my personal treatment choice is an integrated approach. Had I not left the educational field to study biology and neurology, however, I may never have realized the interrelatedness of various parts to the whole, or the importance of combining therapies. I may not ever have seen the bigger picture, remaining blind to what is actually going on when an individual cannot seem to learn according to the way I was trained to teach. The fact is that the human body has a number of different systems, including the nervous system, the immune system, the digestive system, and the circulatory system. The cells within these systems communicate with each other and can help each other. When therapies are integrated, all systems in the body may benefit and be restored to function optimally. This idea is as true for the treatment of dyslexia as it is for the treatment of any ailment. As previously explained, dyslexia is typically not a one-system issue. For example, notice the increased incidence of allergies, immune system problems, and musculoskeletal issues among dyslexics.

Instead of addressing the myriad symptoms dyslexics display, traditional treatment of dyslexia generally considers only the reading problem, dissecting the issue of phonemes and graphemes, which is just the tip of the iceberg. But one system affects another—it's the way humans are designed—and ultimate success in the reversal of dyslexia requires a whole-body approach. Problems with parts of the body that may seem unrelated to learning may, in fact, result in learning difficulties. The confusion that dyslexics associate with the written word can also show up in speech, gait, and coordination. Everything is connected, and without strong neurological and structural foundations, some systems of the body will not be able to do their jobs effectively. They may work, but not as well as they should.

If you have a child with dyslexia, remember that there are no quick fixes when it comes to fostering positive physical and intellectual growth. Change takes time, and developments must occur in the proper order. A thorough, comprehensive approach to treatment will save you time, money, and heartache. Dealing with the superficial layer of a learning disorder without looking at the deeper levels can lead to frustration, cynicism, and confusion. Even compensation techniques may cease to work. Rather than feeling hopeless because one therapy did not fix the entire pattern of symptoms associated with dyslexia, it may be time to attack the problem on many levels, starting at its most basic.

Working from the Bottom Up

Dyslexia is a disorder that needs to be tackled from the bottom up. The reptilian brain must be addressed first. This primitive layer of the brain requires a sense of calm and safety in order to take in and process outside information correctly. Creating a peaceful and secure environment for a dyslexic person is important. Of course, there are many possible reasons behind a brain that reverts to survival mode, particularly if it is a child's brain. Stress in the home, a fast-paced environment, too much time in front of the television, and even a head injury can place the brain in a reactive state in which it becomes very difficult to learn new concepts. A child whose reptilian brain predominates may also have trouble sleeping, suffer from nightmares, or often seem anxious. Once the reptilian brain is calmed, physical, structural, and sensory-motor issues should be treated with whichever techniques might apply to the patient, promoting therapeutic synergy.

From a developmental point of view, crawling, climbing, and twirling in circles all help reorganize muscles and nerves, encouraging a better sense of gravity and spatial intelligence. This bottom-up process is critical to the eventual reversal of dyslexia. Movement from the large muscle groups in the body "greases the wheels" of the brain so that it might engage in speaking and reading correctly. Therapies that address physical movements that affect balance and coordination are usually performed by occupational therapists, but may also be adopted by parents and teachers, and include Sensory Integration, Books Neural Therapy, Brain Gym, and Interactive Metronome. Even playing a musical instrument, enjoying a lively game of ping-pong, or learning a martial art can help coordinate gross and fine motor skills. These skills, in turn, improve brain function.

In addition to treating sensory-motor glitches and neurological timing issues, it is crucial to consider immune system function, nutrition, and allergies, all of which can affect the ability to learn. Years ago, there was a time when I might turn to the mother of one of my patients and say, "Now it's time to send your child to the allergy doctor." Mom might roll her eyes and say, "One more doctor? I don't have enough time the way as it is. How am I supposed to squeeze in one more doctor appointment after school?" Due to this common reaction to an integrated approach, I soon decided to have as many therapies available in my office as possible—one-stop shopping, so to speak. Sometimes you have to bite the bullet and, for a few months or more, make time and rearrange priorities to focus on all the puzzle pieces of dyslexia. By dealing with each piece, the combination of therapies will build a strong, cohesive framework for learning.

Stepping Into My Office

Finding a professional who understands the importance of an integrated approach can be an intimidating task. Knowing what to look for during a first meeting can be extremely helpful. The questions asked and tests requested by a therapist often signal whether treatment will address every aspect of the problem. Because I personally approach therapy as a collection of integrated techniques, I thought it might be helpful to describe the way in which I begin the process of treatment in my practice.

Before a patient even shows up at my office, I generally inquire about the individual's physical and emotional health, as well as the physical and emotional health of the patient's family members. I ask about the patient's birth, including whether there might have any complications during delivery. I inquire about immune system function, known allergies, and vaccination history. I investigate nutrition, asking what foods the patient eats and how these foods are prepared. I inquire about the patient's school and social history, as well as which hobbies the patient enjoys or avoids.

During the first office visit, I conduct a structural and neurological exam, looking for various physical misalignments or other neurological quirks that can affect learning. I often request further tests to check for possible heavy metal and mineral imbalances, neurotransmitter problems, and allergies. I may prescribe pre- and post-therapy tests of reading, writing, and math skills, as well as a motor proficiency exam, depending on the examples of ability that the patient has brought in advance. When there is any indication of ADHD accompanying the dyslexia, I also include a computerized attention and focus pre- and post- therapy test. I may even ask the patient to keep a food diary for three to seven days.

Based on the test results, I'll come up with a well-rounded strategy designed to help each of the various involved systems. I may do just the Books Neural Therapy, which addresses the structural and neurological deficits that often accompany dyslexia. Frequently, I will integrate allergy desensitization, emotional de-stressing techniques, and neurofeedback into the sessions. I may suggest adding fish oils or other nutritional aids to the diet. Occasionally, I may suggest a consultation with a homeopath or an EFT practitioner as a way of speeding up emotional changes, or with a developmental optometrist to see if the patient needs eyeglasses. Oftentimes, with permission, I will confer with other professionals and tutors who have already worked with the patient. It all depends on the individual. And this is exactly the point. If a therapist does not seem to show any interest in viewing dyslexia as a whole-body issue, with its presence in many systems, which is unique to each patient, it is likely time to seek a different therapist.

Unfortunately, a traditionally trained medical doctor or psychologist is likely to be a specialist and may not necessarily be aware of other helpful modalities. Most doctors are trained to try one treatment, switching it only if it is not working. A child-friendly, holistic, alternative, comprehensive, complementary health and wellness center, on the other hand, will often offer a well-rounded approach to treatment, even if it includes several different therapists overseen by one person. As mentioned earlier, word of mouth, whether attained online or in person, can be a great help when searching for the right therapist for your situation.

> *"Your life changes when you have a working knowledge of your brain. It takes guilt out of the equation when you recognize that there's a biological basis for certain issues. On the other hand, you won't be left feeling helpless when you see how you can influence that biology."*
>
> —JOHN RATEY, SPARK: THE REVOLUTIONARY NEW SCIENCE OF EXERCISE AND THE BRAIN[5]

Rearranging Your Life

After all the decisions have been made regarding therapists and treatment, most patients, or parents of a patient, wonder how long their lives will need to be rearranged in order to successfully reverse dyslexia. Over the years, I have found that the initial phase of therapy usually lasts about three months. This first duration of integrative therapy is usually the most intensive and dramatic. Patients typically alternate through periods of growth and plateaus, but the majority of people will find one round of therapy sufficient. Other patients, however, based on a number of factors, progress more slowly and require more time. For example, in the case of children of preschool age until the age of six or seven, neurological changes need more time to become fully integrated within the system as a whole before improvements in school performance may be seen.

CONCLUSION

Brain science has advanced more quickly in the last ten years than ever before in modern medical history. There are now many ways to measure brain activity and gather data about learning itself. The old methods of approaching dyslexia gave an incomplete picture of the disorder, in both definition and treatment. They typically focused on higher brain function, leading to incorrect conclusions. It is no wonder no progress was being made in the treatment of dyslexia; the model itself was flawed. Recent scientific breakthroughs, however, show the complex web of inter -

actions that take place throughout the body. Advances in biology, physics, and neuroscience prove that the brain is capable of changing, rebuilding, and upgrading itself at any age.

Unfortunately, it is with a heavy heart that I tell you that you are now more informed than many of the people who make daily decisions regarding healthcare and educational policy. Although numerous safe and effective alternative treatments have been available for over a decade, most teachers and clinicians remain unaware of these options and the scientific rationale for their use. Those traditionally based professionals who are aware of alternative therapies simply say there is not enough evidence or research to support these techniques. They often recommend that patients stick with tried and true methods, even though, clearly, traditional means have not reversed the problem of dyslexia.

Dyslexia is not just about reading. There are many facets to this condition, so it must be treated in a multifaceted way. Because dyslexia affects multiple systems, it requires multiple types of therapy. Its roots can often be found deep in the most primitive layer of the brain. Traditional treatment takes a top-down approach, focusing on upper-level brain function. This perspective leads to superficial results and encourages compensatory tricks and workarounds; it does not reverse the problem. When therapy goes deeper, the neurological system can be reorganized, timing and sequencing issues can be corrected, and dyslexia can often be permanently remedied. A thorough, comprehensive plan that includes neurological, emotional, environmental, and even nutritional components will save you time, money, and heartache.

If you have a child with dyslexia, it is vitally important that you be your child's advocate when discussing therapy with your healthcare provider. Armed with this new knowledge of dyslexia, you can help find the right combination of treatments that will allow your child to fully engage in life, actively thriving instead of defensively reacting to the world. Only you can give your child unconditional love and make decisions that will effect crucial changes at the deepest level. These choices are yours to make, and you need not feel insecure about asking for a truly integrated approach. On the contrary, your child's success in life may depend on your doing so.

5.

The Importance of Nutrition

"Mommy, can we buy these?" asked the five-year-old girl standing next to her mother. I could not help but overhear her as we stood in line at the checkout counter of a shop at the airport. The little girl was holding four different bags of candy. Her mother, looking tired and bedraggled, agreed without blinking an eye, and then proceeded to buy a pastry and a soda for herself. I was witnessing firsthand what goes on every day in the lives of so many people: Quick solutions win out over good nutrition.

When people are too tired to go food shopping, cook, or organize a well-balanced meal, they will typically opt for fast food or unhealthy snacks. Unfortunately, parents who have a child with a learning disorder such as dyslexia often feel particularly overwhelmed and exhausted. They may simply wish to sit down in front of the television with their child, not think about anything, and eat whatever can be easily grabbed. Although "vegging out" in this way may provide a brief respite to these parents, it is not the solution to the real issue. If you are reading this book, I know you are looking for solutions. Fear not. They are closer than you think, but to achieve them you must recognize your personal responsibility in the long-term success of dyslexia reversal. If you are unwilling or unable to put all or some of the following nutritional suggestions into practice, you may be wasting your time and money on therapy, no matter which program you choose.

As a parent of a dyslexic child, you might think that nutritional considerations can fall by the wayside once the learning disorder has been reversed and your son or daughter is reading and writing at an appropriate grade level. Allowing your child to eat candy or drink soda instead of sticking to healthful foods often amounts to the path of least resistance, which will always be a very tempting choice. And food can't possibly have that much effect once you've accomplished the incredible task of reversing dyslexia, right? Actually, this belief is absolutely wrong, and falling back into old dietary habits can set a child back at square one. Proper nutrition is a vital key to an individual thriving throughout a lifetime. It should not be approached as a temporary necessity but rather embraced as a permanent change in mindset.

EMBRACING A NEW MINDSET

Changing a daily diet involves a big shift not only in eating habits but also in perspective. Meals need to be regarded in a different way—one that highlights how important wholesome nutrition is to both body and mind. Most people say they are too busy to cook meals for the family on a regular basis, so they end up buying the quickest, easiest food options with little thought given to their nutritional content, but it does not have to be this way. Recipe planning, focused grocery shopping, and a little advance preparation can make a healthful diet achievable, while also saving you both time and money. These small adjustments can also help you make better last-minute food choices and have more nutritious snacks at your fingertips.

In addition to their nutritional significance, food preparation and eating have important communal aspects. Meals offer a time when everyone can come together to talk, share, and enjoy each other's company. Being labeled dyslexic can be an isolating experience, especially for a child. Sharing family experiences at mealtimes can be extremely beneficial to a dyslexic individual's self-esteem, confidence, and self-worth. People are nourished not only by food but also by each other's presence when sitting around the supper table.

If you are a parent, nurturing and feeding your child is one of your main responsibilities. It comes with the job. While public schools certainly have a role to take very seriously when it comes to what children eat, parents should understand that a healthful mindset starts at home. The food habits children learn at home will positively influence how they think about food for the rest of their lives. All parents need to find the time to focus on nutritious food. (You'll notice I didn't say expensive food; I simply said nutritious. Beans and rice are inexpensive, easy to make, and loaded with nutrition.) Time spent on good meals will yield major benefits. A well-behaved, well-adjusted child is worth the investment.

By adopting worthwhile dietary ideas and encouraging them to become long-term lifestyle changes, therapies such as those that help reverse learning disorders can remain permanently successful. Reverting to previous unhealthful eating habits, however, may cause the benefits of treatment to disappear. Think of the matter as you would an automobile: You can repair the engine, but if you keep putting sugar in the gas tank, the car is not going to run right, and will be back in the shop in no time.

THE BIG FOUR FOOD PROBLEMS

When it comes to learning disorders and nutrition, changes in diet should start with avoidance of certain foods. While sugar used to be the main culprit in connection with attention issues and learning problems, most nutritionists have found it necessary to broaden the list to four items: wheat, dairy, sugar, and caffeine. In recent years, food allergies and sensitivities, which can play a part in learning troubles, have often been associated with dairy and wheat products, while ingredients such as sugar and caffeine have been linked with other troubling physiological changes that can negatively affect learning. Eliminating these big four items from a dyslexic's diet can be a very effective way to keep the disorder at bay. Is this a simple idea? Yes. Is it an easy idea to put into practice? No. But once this adjustment has been made, it will likely produce amazingly positive changes in the behavior and ability of your dyslexic child, not to mention the rest of the family.

I know, I know. I like these big four items, too. But truthfully, I like performing at my highest level much better than the temporary pleasure I receive by eating any of these foods. Sometimes people can eat these foods in moderate amounts, and sometimes they cannot. Once you and your family have successfully abstained from these four items for a while, you may gradually reintroduce them into the daily routine one by one to see the effects they might cause, building meals from there.

Wheat

A main ingredient in what is known as the "staff of life," or bread, wheat is not as nutritious as it was in biblical days. It now contains 30 percent more gluten, the gluey protein present in wheat and wheat-related grains, including rye and barley. Since the advent of modern strains of wheat grain, the number of people with gluten allergies and celiac disease (an autoimmune disease of the small intestine caused by gluten) has increased sharply. One of the alarming facts regarding this trend is that a person can be sensitive to gluten for years and have no symptoms at all, while the lining of the gut slowly becomes compromised, potentially leading to various ailments.

Eliminating wheat and wheat-related grains means that pizza, bread, cereal, pasta, and many types of cracker will need to be avoided. Yes, I know your kids live on "goldfish" treats for snacking after school. Yes, I know you have pizza several times a week. Yes, I know you are probably wondering how to get rid of wheat without your family feeling as though it is being penalized and left without any choices. Take a breath. I've coached many people through this change. By the end of three weeks, you'll probably be bragging to your friends and coworkers about your diet. (Other people may even ask you for advice on how to make the adjustment.) The fact is that wheat substitutes are much easier to find now than they were only a few years ago. Gluten-free eating is becoming very well known. Because of this rise in awareness, grocery stores often have gluten-free sections, and even restaurants have begun to identify gluten-free choices on their menus.

Wheat Alternatives

Instead of having bread with a meal, try potatoes or rice. If you must have bread, explore gluten-free types made with quinoa, millet, or chickpea flour. If you wish to bake your own bread, cakes, or cookies, you can buy gluten-free flour at most health food stores, some grocery stores, or online. For pasta lovers, numerous companies offer gluten-free noodles. Rice noodles are often found in the Chinese section of a grocery store. Rice flour may also be used to make rice crackers, which are a good substitute for wheat crackers. Even gluten-free pizza crust has become widely available in most places.

Comprehensive lists of gluten-containing foods may be found online, which will help you learn the items to avoid in your diet. Some may surprise you. For instance, did you know that soy sauce has wheat in it? Not to worry, though. Tamari is a version of soy sauce that contains little to no wheat (consult the bottle for ingredients) and can be readily found at most grocery stores.

Dairy

Like wheat, dairy is a common dietary allergen. A dairy allergy is caused by a group of proteins known as casein, which is found in mammalian milk. Casein is much like the gluten in wheat, in that the protein is hard to break down and can cross the blood brain barrier and travel from the intestines to the brain. These proteins are so similar that many products are advertised as "gluten-free, casein-free."

Staying away from dairy foods can be very tough, but if you can do it for three weeks, you may be amazed at the difference a non-dairy diet can make to physical and psychological health. You'll be surprised by the amount of mucous problems that clear up when dairy is eliminated from a diet. Runny noses, ear infections, and sinus headaches can all be manifestations of too much dairy. While many of the tastiest foods contain dairy, there are now many great substitutes in this area.

Dairy Alternatives

Almond milk, rice milk, and coconut milk are all good alternatives to cow's milk. There are several nondairy ice creams available, even at your local grocery store. While there are numerous cheese substitutes out there, be careful when choosing one, and read labels. Casein is often still an ingredient in cheese replacements. To make a good cheese substitute for casseroles or other dishes in which you might use shredded cheese, grind macadamia nuts in a food processor or coffee grinder. Macadamia nuts become creamy in texture when processed. Cashew nuts may also work well. For a snack that has a similar texture to crackers and cheese, try eating crackers and sliced avocado.

Sugar

Ask any eye doctor about the relationship between vision and blood sugar disruptions caused by diabetes or hypoglycemia and you will learn that fluctuations in blood sugar levels can, in fact, change a patient's eye prescription. In addition, there is evidence that sugar may cause some of the bones that form the eye socket to slide out of their proper positions just a tiny bit. This tiny bit of displacement, however, is enough to disrupt the muscles and nerves involved in vision and reading. This phenomenon is exactly what happened in the case mentioned in Chapter One. (See page 19.) After the patient had eaten large quantities of sugary foods, her sphenoid bone and the surrounding muscles lost their ability to maintain their proper positions, preventing her brain from seeing and processing written information correctly.[1]

The human brain requires sugar to function, but not the refined table sugar found today, and certainly not in the amount currently consumed on average. Approximately 100 hundred years ago, the average person consumed a little less than 100 pounds of sugar over a lifetime. Today, Americans consume over 100 pounds of sugar per year. Sugar accounts for 25 to 45 percent of the typical American diet, and drinking soda is the most common way that sugar is ingested.

The human sweet tooth is actually an evolutionary trait. In prehistoric times, it was beneficial for humans to crave naturally sweet edibles such as fruit because these foods were not poisonous. Sugar content essentially equaled survival. Although this trait is not of much use in the modern world, it remains. With sugar so plentiful these days, what was once a helpful characteristic is now a detriment to human health.

The food industry knows that people are more likely to continue to purchase a product if that product contains sugar, so sugar is added in places you might never suspect. A common practice is to feed sugar to animals before slaughter to improve the color and flavor of the meat. Hamburgers may have corn syrup added to reduce shrinkage and improve their flavor. French fries have sugar added to deepen their color during the frying process. Sugar is in hot dogs, salad dressing, frozen pizza, peanut butter and, of course, ketchup. In fact, there are hundreds of "standardized" foods, including canned vegetables, vanilla extract, baby formula, and iodized salt, which are not required to list the amount of sugar they contain.

Sugar Alternatives

The best way to avoid sugar is to eat foods in as close to their natural states as possible. When an item is processed, it is likely sugar has been added. Instead of drinking juice, eat the whole fruit; the cellulose in fruit slows the metabolism of sugar in the body. If you still wish to drink juice, dilute it with water to cut your sugar intake.

Remember that honey, maple syrup, and molasses are essentially sugar as well. They are not as processed as table sugar, but they will eventually be broken down in a similar fashion by the body. (Molasses, however, is loaded with beneficial minerals, particularly iron. People with low iron stores can build up iron levels by eating molasses daily.) In recent years, agave, the nectar of the agave plant, has become a popular sweetener. Agave is sweeter than table sugar, which may cause people to use less of it, but it is still sugar. Another plant-based sweetener is stevia, which seems to have virtually no effect on blood sugar level. While it may be a great sugar substitute, overindulging in any sweetener will only hinder achievement of the ultimate goal, which is to become accustomed to eating less sugary foods.

Finally, when people seem to crave sugar, many times they really want fat or protein. Instead of going for that candy bar, try an avocado or guacamole. An avocado is very satisfying, has great texture, and leaves you feeling full, thanks to its content of healthy fat. A good protein will also give you sustained energy without spiking your blood sugar level like sugar.

Caffeine

Caffeine acts a bit like sugar, in that it elevates energy levels only to lead to fatigue after its effects have worn off. It results in a wonderful high followed by a troublesome low a few hours later. Caffeine has also been linked to mood swings, irritability, hyperactivity, and aggressive behavior, all of which have been implicated in learning challenges. These effects temporarily divert the user from focusing their mind, paying attention, and learning effectively.

Eliminating caffeine means avoiding coffee, tea, caffeinated soft drinks, and most certainly energy drinks. You may wonder how you will ever be able to abstain from coffee or keep your kids away from soda for an extended period of time. While going cold turkey is one way to tackle the caffeine problem, doing so may result in sluggish behavior, sleepiness, and resistance. For some people, weaning slowly off caffeine is easier to do. Cutting down on caffeine consumption over a week or two can help alleviate the headaches and grumpy behavior that accompany quitting caffeine. Taking extra B vitamins can provide extra energy and a positive outlook during the transition. (Do not take B vitamins in the late afternoon, as they may make it hard to fall asleep at night.) Exercising more during this time can raise your level of dopamine, a feel-good chemical in the brain, which encourages a more positive and balanced perspective. Exercise also improves sleep.

THE IMPORTANCE OF BREAKFAST

Imagine a child whose typical breakfast consists of sugar-laden prepackaged cereal, cow's milk, a sprinkle of sugar, and maybe fruit juice or chocolate milk. This child is going to be supercharged by all that sugar in the morning and hard to settle into a seat. By the afternoon, a slump will set in. This child will soon have trouble focusing, paying attention, and learning. In regards to older kids, inappropriate breakfasts are also much too common amongst junior and senior high school students. There are an increasing number of high school students lined up at the local coffee shop for their triple espressos with sugar and milk. During the teenage years, fitting in with peers becomes enormously important, so breaking bad habits can be tough. Once children recognize how much better healthful foods make them feel, willpower should improve.

An adequate amount of protein at breakfast is important because it helps sustain energy levels throughout the day without the highs and lows that accompany doughnuts, sugary cereals, and pastries. An excellent protein choice is eggs, which can be served in a variety of ways. Eggs are much easier to digest if they aren't overcooked.

Smoothies are quick to prepare, can be eaten while in the car or on the go, and can be loaded with added nutrients. Start with a good protein powder such as hemp protein, add some fruit (or even spinach, if you can handle the color it makes the drink) and a dose of omega-3 fish oil, pour in some almond milk (rice milk

Water

Water is one of the most important fuels for the brain, as it allows information to be transported across synapses. Caffeine dehydrates the body and brain, which is why it is important to drink two glasses of water for each cup of coffee you consume. Even the cerebral spinal fluid (CSF) that surrounds the spine and brain can get dehydrated. Caffeine also depletes your body of B vitamins, which help keep your energy level high and your mood positive. Simply put, drinking water instead of caffeinated soda or coffee is one of the best adjustments people can make to their dietary routines.

or coconut milk can also be used as the base), and blend. If you wish to add raw eggs to a smoothie, I suggest using organic eggs.

Oatmeal or any other hot cereal is another great choice. If you have a crock-pot, you can even prepare the oatmeal the night before so that it is ready by morning. Add a dash of cinnamon and a handful of raisins for a delicious meal. The aroma is great, and the warmth of the cereal is very comforting during the winter months.

Although it is not commonly eaten for breakfast in the United States, soup is one of my personal morning favorites. A nice vegetable or chicken broth with lots of added veggies or cooked legumes makes a hearty meal. I actually make a batch of soup during my weekly food preparation so that I can have a bowl ready in a flash each morning.

NURTURING VERSUS NUTRITION

Despite parents' best intentions, some nurturing habits may be negatively influencing their children's nutrition. As long as sugary foods have been easily accessible, they have also been a substitute for proper nurturing and an unfortunate source of comfort in Western culture. Adults often eat items such as candy and chocolate to feel better, and children are frequently offered similar sweets as a motivator or soother. Such a tactic may produce the desired result, but the effect is always short-lived. When the good feeling associated with sugary foods wears off, most people begin to want these treats more and more. It is a road that can quickly lead to a generally poor diet, which, as explained earlier, plays a role not only in weight issues but also in learning disorders.

Effectively nurturing a child requires a level of dedication, patience, and emotional strength that may seem impossible to reach at times. In truth, there are no real short cuts when it comes to raising a child (although it is perfectly understandable to wish there were). Throughout all the years I have been treating learning-challenged individuals, I have watched children from vastly different economic, social, and racial backgrounds succeed in overcoming their problems. The one common factor behind these successes was a parent who was willing to go the distance and do what needed to be done. Parents must provide their children not only with a safe and stable environment but also with the right foods to promote brain function, clarity of thought, and an ability to learn. It is tempting to comfort or reward a child with candy, but doing so would be sabotaging treatment and long-term success.

The best way to ensure that worrying about nutrition does not overtake your life is simply to have a pantry and refrigerator stocked with healthful items (and devoid of unwholesome items). This way, when you run to grab a snack or need to prepare a meal, your only options will be good ones. To accomplish this task, you may need some advice on where to shop, what to buy, what to avoid, how to read labels, and what snacks are a good choice when the time comes to reward or comfort your child (or simply to have a snack). Once you have learned how to surround yourself and your family with good food, you will not have to think about how to eat well. It will have become second nature.

Where to Shop

The best and most nutritious food will be locally grown, which can be found at your local farmer's market or taken from your own garden. Organic groceries are the next best choice in shopping, and may be the best option for city dwellers. Organic produce and meat can cost almost double the price of their non-organic counterparts, but they are not treated with the potentially harmful chemicals that non-organic options are. Even a bulk chain like Costco realizes that people want organic food choices and offers many excellent organic fresh and frozen vegetables and fruit, as well as organic meat. The most common place to shop is your neighborhood grocery store. Thankfully, many of your average grocery stores have begun stocking organic choices, particularly in metropolitan areas. Many also offer gluten-free foods.

When shopping in your local grocery store, steer your cart around the perimeter of the store where the fresh and refrigerated foods are. Avoid the tempting aisles that contain candy, prepackaged foods, and soda. Once you've finished shopping around the perimeter of the store, head to the frozen food section for the veggies and fruit you were not able to find fresh. While the process of packaging degrades the nutrients somewhat, vegetables that are destined for the frozen aisle are generally picked at their best and flash-frozen in a still very nutritious state. Finally, if you wish to buy canned produce, avoid those with added sugar or salt. Both items are frequently added to preserve shelf life.

What to Buy

While there are a few obvious foods that should take top spots on your grocery list, there are quite a few items to seek out when trying to feed the body and brain properly. As recently mentioned, fresh or frozen organic vegetables and fruit are a must, while organic meat should be your choice if you are a meat-eater. Fresh or frozen wild fish is very good choice, though even canned is a decent option.

Nuts, with all their good fats, can support a strong body and brain, but most commercially available nuts are roasted in unhealthy oils and contain additives, so choose them in the raw. When it comes to nutritious snacks, pick up sunflower seeds, pumpkin seeds, dried fruit (from the bulk bin, as these are less likely to contain preservatives), and rice crackers or cakes. (See page 90 for snack ideas.)

If you are trying to wean your child off soda, opt for unsweetened pineapple, apple, or grape juice instead. Be sure to dilute the juice with a bit of water to cut the sweetness, raising the amount of water in the drink until your child is accustomed to plain water. Do not replace a soda habit with a juice habit, as these choices still have natural sugars. If your child wishes fruit flavor, it is best to offer a piece of fruit rather than a glass of juice. The fiber contained in raw fruit helps slow the body's absorption of sugar, preventing a sugar jolt. Remember, the body always prefers food in its most natural state.

As a replacement for cow's milk, pick up some almond, rice, or even coconut milk. They are all great substitutes. Soy milk is also a good alternative, but be sure your child does not have a soy allergy before choosing this option. If soy milk is your choice, go for a product made with non-genetically modified soy beans.

Finally, add organic varieties of grains like rice, quinoa, oats, and millet to your shopping list, and decrease the amount of wheat and spelt products you purchase, as they may cause inflammation.

What to Avoid

In terms of what to avoid while grocery shopping, the big four ingredients have already been mentioned, but the following may give you a more detailed picture of the items to cross off your list. Prepackaged and processed foods of all kinds, of course, are not recommended. Processed, smoked, or cured meats like bacon, sausages, and hot dogs are also not good choices, as they often contain milk, corn, sugar, and numerous food additives. While peanut butter is not off the list, most commercial peanut butters are loaded with sugar. Steer clear of these types and seek out a pure organic peanut butter. Some grocery stores even allow you to make your own on the premises.

As previously explained, non-organic fruit and vegetables may contain high levels of chemical pesticides and should be avoided. Sometimes, however, there are no organic options. In this case, it is good to know which vegetables and fruits generally contain the highest levels of pesticides, so you can avoid them at the very least. These items include:

- Apples
- Blueberries
- Celery
- Grapes
- Green beans
- Peaches
- Pears
- Potatoes
- Spinach
- Strawberries

If your local grocery store does not stock organic produce, simply opt for the fruits and vegetables that do not appear on this list.

How to Read Labels

While ideally you will not be buying much of anything that comes in a package, it is unreasonable to assume that absolutely nothing of what you buy will have an ingredient label. Therefore, it is crucial to understand how to read these labels and decode the technical words they may contain. It is important to know that the ingredients on a label are listed in order of amount. The most plentiful substance is the first ingredient listed, and so on. It is also important to know that commercial food companies may very cleverly disguise certain ingredients you know to avoid by calling them different, unfamiliar names.

Sugar may actually be listed several times on a list of ingredients, each time under a different name, but it is all still sugar. The many names of sugar include:

- Barley malt
- Beet sugar
- Brown sugar
- Buttered syrup
- Cane sugar
- Caramel
- Corn syrup
- Corn syrup solids

- Date sugar
- Dextrose
- Ethyl maltol
- Fructose
- Fruit juice
- Fruit juice concentrate
- Glucose
- Glucose solids
- Golden syrup
- Grape sugar
- High fructose corn syrup

- Lactose
- Malt syrup
- Maltodextrin
- Maltose
- Mannitol
- Molasses
- Raw sugar
- Refiner's syrup
- Sorbitol
- Sucrose

While some labels may list common sugar substitutes such as aspartame, saccharin, and sucralose, I do not endorse ingesting these artificial sweeteners either.

Another cleverly disguised ingredient is a flavor enhancer known as monosodium glutamate, or MSG. Like table salt, this substance is a savory additive that is known to increase palatability of food and possibly encourage overeating. There are also some people who have displayed a particular sensitivity to MSG, so it is a good idea to know its other names in case they appear on a label. These other names include:

- Autolyzed plant protein
- Autolyzed yeast
- Glutamate
- Glutamic acid
- Hydrolyzed plant protein (HPP)

- Hydrolyzed vegetable protein (HVP)
- Monopotassium glutamate
- Senomyx
- Textured protein
- Vegetable protein extract
- Yeast extract

Make a game of reading labels. Think of yourself as a label detective. If you have kids, get them involved. For example, give a small prize to the one who finds the most kinds of sugar on a label. Children will surprise and delight you with their willingness to eat good foods once they've taken part in reading labels.

Nevertheless, it can still be a pain to have to decipher information every time you want to eat. Ultimately, it may actually be less time-consuming and more enjoyable to visit the produce section once a week, buy whole foods, chop them up, and put them into little snack baggies so that healthy snacks are readily available whenever you or your child wants one.

Snack Choices

Everyone loves a good snack, but children may be the biggest snackers of all. Healthful snack options are important in any household, but particularly so to a family that is working towards reversing a learning disorder. The easiest way to know that a snack is nutritious is to prepare it at home. Getting the children involved in the process of snack preparation is a wonderful way to get them interested in what they will be eating, while also teaching them about nutrition. Kids who are involved in most any educational process are more likely to comply because they feel included and connected.

Sliced and diced veggies and fruits are great snacks. Try dipping apples, celery, or carrots in peanut butter, almond butter, or hummus. Guacamole is another wonderful choice. This avocado-based dip contains an abundance of healthy fat and makes a great companion to crackers and veggies. You can even incorporate these new snack ideas into your everyday life by keeping a cooler in the car. Keep the snacks in the cooler so that they are available when you are out and about.

You can also make your own trail mix and package individual servings in little snack bags. This is another task that you and your children can do together. It can be a lot of fun to go to the bulk section of the grocery store to select raisins, dried cranberries, nuts, sunflower seeds, and whatever else you might like to include in your mix.

Although you may not know it, popcorn is a fine snack. Yes, there is nothing wrong with popcorn as long as it is not soaked in too much salt, butter, or sugary syrup. It is an especially fun snack if you pop it yourself. Like trail mix, you can package it in snack bags that the children can take to school or on trips.

When you are tired of these snack ideas, go online and search for new ones. There is no shortage of helpful resources out there. You can even see if there are any parent groups that regularly meet to discuss diet and nutrition in your area. Parents who have children with food allergies or sensitivities sometimes organize get-togethers to talk about meal plans and snacks. These groups can provide new information and ideas.

If you cannot find a group to join, start one yourself. Other parents would probably love to take part. You do not have to figure it all out on your own.

Getting the Kids Involved

As a parent, you can do no better service to your children than to involve them in your family's diet. At the grocery store, while going down the produce aisle, have the kids choose vegetables of various colors. Having foods of many colors on the table each night is a great way of getting good nutrition and keeping it interesting. In addition, allow the children to help out in the kitchen. Measuring foods is a great way to practice math skills, as it provides a real-world use for tools such as multiplication, division, and fractions. You can also let your kids decorate their own aprons—whatever encourages them to make the idea of nutrition feel like their own. From the age of seven, each of my kids was in charge of one meal per week for the family. While in college, my daughter said that was one of the best chores I ever made her do.

Finally, you could start a kids' food club. Invite the children in your neighborhood over for food and fun play dates. Have the kids create the snacks themselves, perhaps according to a theme, and have a fun outdoor activity planned as well. The more a child feels connected to good eating habits, the more likely those habits are to take root.

Rules of Thumb

While the study of nutrition is complex, there are a few good rules of thumb to learn that will help keep you on the road to better eating habits. When it comes to choosing the right foods, the main guidelines are the following:

- If it rots, it is probably good for you. The fact that it can rot means it has no preservatives or additives—as opposed to a snack food such as Twinkies, which has a shelf life of nine years.

- If it comes from a plant, eat it. If it is made in a factory, do not eat it.

- Eat food that is in as close to its natural state as possible.

- If you leave a food outside and no insects go near it, do not eat it.

- Avoid sugar-free and fat-free foods. These terms simply mean that someone did something to the food that is not natural. These products will typically have extra artificial additives to give them the taste and texture normally provided by the fat and sugar.

- Stay away from foods with ingredients you cannot pronounce.

Here's the thing about eating well: You can put in the time now or lose the time later. If you put in the time to learn better eating habits now, you and your family will reap benefits that can last a lifetime. If you would rather cut corners and choose the quick and easy diet path of processed foods and sugary treats, you and your family will likely lose a number of years to physical ailments and cognitive problems down the line.

As author Michael Pollan says, "Eat food. Not too much. Mostly plants. . . . That, more or less, is the short answer to the supposedly incredibly complicated and confusing question of what we humans should eat in order to be maximally healthy."[12]

CONCLUSION

Recall that many brain problems actually start in the gut. Thankfully, they are also correctable. In 400 BC, Hippocrates stated, "Let food be your medicine." Similarly, American Indians have a saying: Water is the first medicine. Needless to say, the concept of the healing power of nutrition has been around a long time. We would do well to listen to our elders regarding this topic. Some things in life are too basic to ignore. These are good sleep, good rest, good water, and good nutrition. Cutting corners in these areas knocks the human system out of balance in the long run, creating physical and mental disorders, and worsening learning problems such as dyslexia.

It is important to encourage a sense of excitement and pleasure around food and nutrition. Healthy attitudes towards food are first modeled to a child at home. The tricky thing is not to substitute junk food for comfort. Many learning-challenged children feel isolated and different, and some find some comfort in poor food choices. If you are the parent of such a child, it is time to take the lead and set the tone in regard to nutrition. It is time to teach through play. The process will become easy before long, and these adjustments will take hold as permanent lifestyle changes.

I understand that the subject of nutrition can be controversial, in that it often hits a raw nerve where people are sensitive and resistant. For your sake and the sake of your child, I ask that you put down your defenses. Change begins with a sure commitment to yourself and your loved ones. Most people do not adapt to change easily, even when they know that doing so will yield numerous benefits. Once you see the effects of good nutrition in your life, you will thank yourself for your decisions. The resultant positive changes in your child's behavior, cooperativeness, and mood (and in your own) will make the effort of eating better more than worth it. Don't be surprised if others ask you to help them accomplish the same miracles in their lives.

6.

Brain Boosters

Parents of dyslexic children often wonder what they can do at home to help treat this condition. Because dyslexia is commonly linked to a number of other behavioral issues, pharmaceuticals are frequently the only remedies given. My prescription, however, is quite different. It involves increasing the focus on three activities: exercise, play, and music. As you know, the ability to learn is strengthened when all the senses are engaged. These activities play a role in the efficient intake of information and are very important to the brain. Thankfully, your kids will be happy to hear that playing, exercising, and being musical are essentially "doctor's orders."

Successful treatment involves more than simply getting a child to pass a spelling test or book report; it equips a child with a sound mind and body. It creates a resilient child who is unafraid of stumbling and able to handle whatever life brings. Its goal is to get to the roots of the issue and make long-lasting positive changes, not to be a compensatory band-aid.

When the brain cannot take in and process information efficiently, its capacity to learn becomes compromised. As explained earlier, engaging in activities that involve body movement and motor planning is important to brain growth and function. In addition, these tasks can also aid in positively reorganizing the connections in the brain of an individual already affected by learning troubles, promoting a reversal of these conditions. If building and nourishing a strong brain and body is the goal, the following three simple brain-boosting activities are some of most important tools needed to achieve it. These methods do not require a doctor's prescription, can be done at home, and—most importantly—are fun.

EXERCISE

Exercise can actually make you smarter. Exercise helps the brain function like a superhighway instead of a winding country road with lots of stops and starts that slow it down. Body movement engages the brain and prepares it to learn.

Early in life, neural pathways related to reading, comprehension, speech, and physical coordination are established in the brain. Between the ages of six months and two years, the brain is actually quite delicate, and this is precisely the time when the reptilian brain and limbic system are forming these important neural connections, which should eventually lead to a properly functioning neocortex. In disorders such as dyslexia, communication between the cerebellum of the reptilian brain and the frontal lobe of the neocortex is faulty. Amazingly, exercise can aid in the repair of such broken lines of communication. In the case of a dyslexic individual, exercise plays a vital part in speeding up the connections between the primitive and modern sections of the brain.

Once the brain's basic building blocks are addressed and neural pathways are strengthened through exercise, you will be amazed at how quickly everything starts to fall into place. Socialization skills will improve, a cooperative spirit will take hold, and issues of poor attitude will ease. If life seems headed down the wrong track due to dyslexia, the express train will soon arrive, avoiding all previous stops that slow down learning.

The Naperville Case

After seeing what a huge impact exercise had on the test scores of children in Naperville, Illinois, Dr. John Ratey was inspired to write the book *Spark*. In 1999, 97 percent of eighth graders in this Chicago suburb were among 230,000 students around the world to take a certain math and science test. In previous years, students from China, Japan, and Singapore overwhelmingly had the top scores. But this particular year, the Naperville kids finished sixth in math and first in science. Coincidentally, they were also some of the fittest kids in the United States, with only 3 percent overweight compared to the national average of 30 percent. What were they doing that was so different from typical American kids?

Amazingly, they had been coming to school an hour early each day to run a mile before the start of academic classes. The physical education department used donated heart monitors to check the children's heart rates during exercise. The coach could actually see how much effort a child was exerting, regardless of running speed. The school counselors witnessed so many positive changes in the children that they now advise students to take their toughest classes right after engaging in exercise, when the brain seems to be working at its best.

"Physical activity is crucial to the way we think and feel. Exercise cues the building blocks of learning in the brain. It affects mood, anxiety and attention; it guards against stress and reverses some of the effects of aging," claims Ratey.[1] Engaging in exercise makes you feel better physically, but moving your muscles also produces proteins that travel into the brain and promote the highest thought processes. Physical activity sparks biological change that encourages brain cells to bind together, allowing the brain to adapt to challenges. This echoes what we know about the neuroplasticity of the brain.

In the old paradigm, mind and body were treated as separate entities. But the new paradigm acknowledges that they work in tandem. In fact, exercise amps up the brain and helps it work better.

Couch Potato Kids

As human beings, we were designed to hunt and gather, but in modern times we have become very sedentary. Learning and memory evolved with the motor skills that allowed our ancestors to track down food. For these ancient relatives, as far as the brain was concerned, if the body was not moving, there was no real need for the high brain function involved in learning. Human development still works on the principle that the more you move, the better your brain works; but humans simply aren't moving as much anymore. We have actually built machines to do our physical work, while we sit all day pushing keys and buttons.

Only 6 percent of high schools in the United States offer a daily physical education class, yet kids are spending an average of five and a half hours a day in front of a screen.[2] According to *Reuters Life!*, however, American children aren't the only couch potatoes in the world. Nearly one-third of children globally spend three hours a day or more watching television or surfing online, according to a study of over 70,000 teens in thirty-four nations.[3] The problem is everywhere, regardless of where people live or how much money they make.

It is important to note that the impact of playing motion-controlled video games, in which the movements of the character on screen mimic the player's actual body movements, is not the same as the impact of exercise, despite what the manufacturers may say. A Swedish study at the University of Gothenburg compared the cognitive impact of running twenty minutes on a treadmill to playing twenty minutes of a sports-style motion-controlled video game at a similar intensity. Running improved cognitive test scores immediately, but playing the sport game did not.[4] In another Swedish study examining over one million eighteen-year-old boys who had recently joined the army, better fitness was correlated with higher IQs, even among identical twins. The fitter the twin, the higher his IQ.[5] The fact is that statistics are popping up everywhere about the connection between physical fitness and the ability to learn. At the University of Illinois, a group of nine-

and ten-year-old children had their brains scanned. The results showed that the fitter kids had better attention and executive control. Even twenty minutes of walking before a test raised children's test scores, no matter if the children were otherwise unfit or overweight.[6]

The brain needs the body's help in the form of exercise. The exciting thing about this realization is that you can actually do something for your dyslexic child, and it won't cost you a cent. You don't have to run a mile before school or work, and you don't have to spend a lot of money. Truthfully, any exercise done at any time will do.

For those dyslexics who also deal with behavioral issues, when it comes to controlling emotions, exercise also helps. The brain produces natural "upper" chemicals called endorphins and enkephalins as a result of exercise. John Ratey's previously mentioned book highlights study after study that suggests that exercise lowers the need for antidepressants, anti-anxiety medications, and drugs that have been designed to enhance focus.

Modeling Regular Exercise

If you want your dyslexic child to reap the cognitive benefits of exercise, all you have to do is model regular exercise. Set an example by doing the exercise yourself. Again, the kind of exercise you do isn't so important. What is important is that you actually do it. When clients ask me which exercise is best to do, I say, "Whichever one you actually do is best." Establish an exercise routine, and then be sure to let your children know how much fun you had and how much better you feel after being active.

If possible, it is a good idea to exercise as a family. Physical activities such as walking in nature or bike riding are great ways to nourish family connection and strengthen hearts and bodies at the same time. Following an exercise regimen as a family is beneficial not only to those members with dyslexia but also to the rest of the unit. It increases the stamina and general health of every person involved. When trying to start an exercise routine, always make sure it is fun. Don't teach your children that exercise is a chore or drudgery. Doing so is a surefire way to ensure that they won't exercise in the future.

PLAY

You can play and learn at the same time. It's true. During play, when you are laughing and seeing or hearing new information, this new information is absorbed without any filters or judgment. This fact is relevant to everyone, but is particularly important to a dyslexic individual, whose learning process is often sabotaged by self-judgment and poor self-esteem. This way of acquiring new information almost feels like cheating or sneaking around because it is more fun than most people would associate with learning.

Play actually helps people learn in many ways. It engages a variety of senses, spurs emotions, bolsters the imagination, and promotes the development of ideas. Although many people discount the power of fun and games, the reality is that they are very good for you. That you don't have to convince children to play is simply a bonus. Ask children what they like to do more than anything else and most will immediately answer, "Play!" It brings them great joy. Play is really the work of children because they learn so much while partaking in it. During play, laughter takes hold, creativity soars, and judgments disappear.

What Kind of Play Is Best?

Every individual should remember the importance of play when learning something new. When a person is stuck in the serious and anxiety-driven "survival mode" of the reptilian brain, there isn't much flexibility in the thought process and learning ceases. Likewise, when a person relies too much on the left-brained, critical thought processes of the neocortex, self-judgment can take over and become paralyzing. During play time, however, the mind is open to new concepts and ideas, and flexible enough to absorb information effortlessly.

Play is best when it is interactive. This does not, however, refer to online gaming with friends. It means being fully engaged with body and mind. It means actively engaging the imagination and combining ideas already experienced with those recently conjured up in the mind. Additionally, outdoor play is important. When children play and explore outdoors, their eyes constantly and dramatically change focus; their vision moves from near to far and all around. These practices help both coordination and learning. In Sweden, attendees of daycare centers where children played outside every day regardless of the weather showed better motor coordination and a better ability to concentrate than another group who played only indoors.[7]

In regard to the outdoors, we often overlook nature as a healing balm for the emotional hardships in a child's life. You'll likely never see a slick commercial for nature therapy, though you would for the latest antidepressant drug. A 2003 survey published in the *Journal of Psychiatric Services* found that the rate at which American children were being prescribed antidepressants had almost doubled in five years; the steepest increase, 66 percent, was among preschool children. Perhaps not coincidentally, a generation ago, kids played outside much more than they do today. Nature truly has a way of bringing a person back into a state of harmony. If you are in a safe area, spending time outside is great emotional therapy.

If you were to ask Jaak Panksepp, author of *Affective Neuroscience*, which type of play is best, he would likely tell you about an experiment he conducted, in which he prescribed "rough-and-tumble play" (RAT) to preschoolers with ADHD tendencies. Amazingly, just twenty minutes of RAT before school led to an increase in the utilization of dopamine in the brain.[8] When the children had lots of this positive natural chemical washing through their bodies, they could then sit still in school for several hours. Compare this rough-and-tumble play solution to the pharmaceutical option, which can come with unwanted side effects. (School nurses have actually complained to me that more and more cabinets are required in their offices simply to contain all the Ritalin-type drugs being administered.) "During play," says Panksepp, "animals are especially prone to behave in flexible and creative ways."[9] When children are drugged to be more compliant, or disciplined too severely for being spontaneous, their natural and healthy instincts are turned off, their enthusiasm, drained.

Of course, a child need not be hyperactive to benefit from play. It is good for everyone. Knowing this fact, it seems a crime to punish children who display unsatisfactory academic skills by making them stay indoors during recess. It is precisely such inactivity that keeps the brain from accomplishing school assignments properly in the first place. Moreover, now the problem is compounded by the negative emotional response to punishment.

Speaking of negative emotional responses, it is important to note that highly competitive games, and the judgment they can

Development through Play

The architects and builders I know often speak of a gut-level understanding of how things fit together. They credit the development of this intuition to the hours of hands-on play in which they took part during childhood. The hand and finger motions used to manipulate toys, puzzles, locks, and other play materials are tied to language development. Coincidentally, motor skills and language areas of the brain are side by side, making it easy to move from one type of task to the other.

Developmentally, humans move the larger muscle groups in a coordinated way—these movements include crawling, walking, and running—and then progress to the use of fine motor skills. These fine motor skills are practiced through such games as pick-up sticks and marbles, painting, and other various arts and crafts projects. While outdoor play is important, games do not always have to take place outside the home. They should, however, spur the imagination and contain some sort of physical aspect to them.

foster, may reduce the joy of play and possibly even shut down parts of the brain. When encouraging play, choose unstructured games, which allow children to interact with their friends and the environment around them, problem solve, and learn social skills without the anxiety and self-doubt that overly competitive play can bring. Unstructured play is how children learn to navigate various social situations gracefully and fluidly. It teaches them how to get along in the world. There is so much knitting and blending that goes on between the various parts of the central nervous system as an individual takes part in playful activities. It is time for society to understand that play is not a luxury; the brain needs it, and a lot of it, every day.

MUSIC

One of the most remarkable ways to help dyslexics is through the use of music. Many progressive therapies include music in their efforts to rewire and improve the brain. It should come as no surprise to know that music has been used as a teaching method for centuries. Nursery rhymes or clever phrases set to rhyme help us remember valuable information. For example, my daughter's formal education began in a Montessori school kindergarten setting, where she learned to write the alphabet by singing a song to go with each letter. Soon she knew all the sounds that each consonant and vowel makes. While still in kindergarten, she began writing me notes and even entire stories.

Rhythm Starts in the Womb

Only in recent years have public school systems stopped using music and rhythm to reinforce learning. Rhythm is important for reading and has benefits that carry over into mathematical and visuospatial learning (visual perception of spatial relationships) as well. Marching and clapping, for example, are easy ways to embed new information deep within the brain. (These activities also reinforce the body's natural affinity for music.) Marching and clapping rhythmically while learning word patterns and math concepts helps the whole body learn and integrate material efficiently and effectively. Rhythm, in fact, encourages proper development even in the womb.

At about sixteen weeks of growth, the embryo hears its mother's heartbeat, which transmits the first rhythms and steady beat patterns. There is a strong correlation between heartbeat and breath, usually to the rhythm of three heartbeats per inhale and three heartbeats per exhale. When you rock a baby to sleep, the repetitive back-and-forth rhythm along with the consistent inhalation and exhalation of breath are reminiscent of the womb, and help quiet and soothe the infant. In addition, the steady rhythm of walking behind a baby's stroller can put an infant to sleep.

Rhythmic training is very important to a child, as a sense of rhythm plays a role in the discrimination of various sounds. Interestingly, the practice of breastfeeding not only nourishes a baby but also places a baby's head close to the mother's heart. By having an ear near mother's breast, a baby learns to assess whether or not its mother is in danger, according to the speed of her heartbeat at the time.[10] Remember, a child senses the safety of a situation first. A learning-challenged child does not necessarily perceive school as a safe place. Musical and rhythmic methods of teaching concepts such as mathematics, reading, and spelling soothe the brain, allowing information to seep in more easily. Repetition, ritual, and rhythm create safety and security, and safety and security encourage learning.

The Sound of Movies

While watching a movie, notice the beat of the drums right before an action scene or moment of intense drama. The beat speeds up and gets louder. This is the movie director's way of manipulating your heartbeat, hopefully raising it so that you feel excited and on the "edge of your seat."

Music and Dyslexia

Music is as old as humankind. It is one of our earliest teachers. Primitive tribes used drums to communicate with other tribes, and Aboriginal Australians still keep their history alive through the musical tradition of the songline. Music helps guide our emotions through such milestones as marriage, death, and birth. It is much more important than most people realize, and can provide tremendous benefits to dyslexics.

As you know, the vestibular system helps establish a person's sense of place in time and space. Rhythm promotes a healthy vestibular system, which encourages smooth and fluid reading. Music sharpens the cerebellum, which acts a tracking station between the reptilian brain, vestibular system, and higher brain functions, and establishes connections with 85 percent of the total brain. The act of singing or playing a musical instrument is immensely helpful when gathering necessary reading skills.

Children with dyslexia are more likely to be slower at decoding sounds of speech and may not hear some of the smaller sounds within words. Singing can help develop these important auditory functions and connect properly processed information to other parts of the brain. The act of singing spends more time on vowel sounds, which dyslexics often have great trouble differentiating, than on consonants. Singing also tends to slow down the parts of speech. In *The Well Balanced Child,* Sally Blythe describes how her son's hearing problem was resolved by his joining a boys' choir. The director actually told her that all his boys tended to improve their reading skills within six months of joining the group, regardless of whether they were formerly good readers or poor readers.[11]

In Denmark, at the end of a one-year study, there was a 70-percent remission in signs of dyslexia after subjects listened to a specific series of music tapes to improve hearing discrimination.[12] At the University of California, spatial intelligence (the ability to perceive the visual world accurately, form mental images of physical objects, and recognize variations of objects), was found to be far higher in preschoolers who had taken eight months of music lessons.[13] According to another study of slow readers, five months of playing a musical instrument, where rhythms could be felt against the body or teeth, increased reading skills by an average of four-and-a-half years.[14,15,16,17,18]

The Suzuki method is a popular way to teach piano and stringed instruments. According to this method, children start lessons at a very young age, with their parents attending the classes. The parent and child listen to the music together repeatedly before the child attempts to play the chosen instrument. Of course, Suzuki is only one method. Any kind of music lessons will help.

If money is an issue, you might be surprised to know that, in my opinion, music lessons should trump tutoring. These days, however, there are many free resources to be found online, so you may not have to choose between one and the other. If you prefer a more personal approach, perhaps you might enlist a musical neighbor to help out.

Finally, you may be wondering whether an older dyslexic individual can benefit from music. The answer is most certainly yes. Treatment that involves music and rhythm is one of best ways to approach dyslexia. Many famous scientists and doctors play a musical instrument to remove their cognitive roadblocks. Einstein was famous for pulling out his violin when he hit a snag in his thought process. Music can foster a bridge between the right and left hemispheres of the brain, allowing them to communicate better. Music tends to release inhibitions, unlocking the brain and opening it up to new ideas.

THE THREE BRAINS

As explained in Chapter 3, there are three levels of the brain, and each is involved in various aspects of learning. Once you understand how exercise, play, and music affect these three brain levels, you can apply these activities optimally to improve reading skills and learning. By discussing these individual areas of the brain one by one, you may be able to take a more focused approach to reversing dyslexia.

The Reptilian Brain

The reptilian brain learns best when exposed to rhythm, routine, repetition, and ritual. As previously noted, nursery rhymes are a great way to impart rhythmic patterns. Playing drums or piano, or almost any instrument, tunes up the sense of rhythm. Even marching or snapping your fingers while learning mathematical facts can help children who are kinesthetic learners. Scarily, many children today cannot pass a steady beat competency test, which is simply a fancy way of saying they cannot clap their hands to the beat of a song.

Repetition is necessary to learn mathematical concepts such as multiplication. Routine provides a sense of comfort and safety. Rituals based around holidays and family events, including songs and games, create a feeling of safety as well. As you know, the reptilian brain needs to be quieted down and feel safe in order to learn. If your dyslexic child is scared on some level, do what you can to foster a sense of security. Cuddle under a blanket or play a quiet game together.

Of course, when the fight-or-flight system of the reptilian brain gets going and adrenaline builds up, another way to discharge this adrenaline is to run. So, even if you or your child cannot run at the time, encourage a walk or run as soon as possible. Exercise is a natural way of changing your body chemistry.

If you decide to eliminate sugar and caffeine from your family's diet, which may be difficult at first, the best way to make the transition is to take B vitamins and exercise more. Movement charges the brain with energy and floods it with dopamine, the "feel-good" chemical. Movement aids concentration, promotes a positive mood, and helps maintain physical health.

The Limbic System

The limbic system deals with human connection, caring, and motivation. Music is a great way of connecting to others, whether listening to it or playing it. Playing games is another way to fos-

ter connections with people. Team play, play dates, and role playing, including acting or drama classes, all bolster social skills and
promote a sense of belonging.

Loneliness and isolation are very stressful to the limbic system—and indeed, the body as whole— and disrupt the learning
process. Being bullied increases a person's feelings of loneliness
and isolation, and unfortunately the Internet is only escalating
this phenomenon. Without adult supervision or face-to-face contact, children can be extremely cruel and hurtful online.

Interestingly, studies show that playing with and caring for a
pet can reduce feelings of isolation and strengthen the limbic system. In fact, boys in juvenile detention homes are sometimes
required to care for horses, and men in prison are sometimes
assigned dogs to train. Having someone depend on you creates
a sense of responsibility and connection. You feel like you matter
to someone, and that someone isn't judging you on your lack
of reading skills. According to authors Adele and Marlena
McCormick, "In the company of a horse, we can learn to develop
that selfless love the Greeks called agape, which leads to a passion
for life—a passion that has dimmed as we've lost our commun-
ion with nature and the natural."[19] As stated by author Larry
Dosey, "In today's high-tech healthcare environment, it is ironic
that a puppy's sloppy kiss can create measurable health benefits,
and that bonding with a horse can create a model, a template that
enables a troubled teen to bond with another person."[20]

Dr. Peter Levine, who developed a therapeutic model for
releasing early trauma from the body, emphasizes the importance of a healthy, integrated nervous system. In his book *Waking the Tiger*, he says, "If we do not sense our connection with all
things, then it is easier to destroy or ignore these things. Human
beings are naturally cooperative and loving. We enjoy working
together. However, without fully integrated brains, we cannot
know about ourselves."[21]

Dan Goleman's classic book *Emotional Intelligence* demon-
strates that how we get along with others is a better predictor of

long-term success than intellect. IQ determines only 4 to 6 percent of future success.[22] Think about this fact for a moment. Success depends on a child's self-worth and relationships more than the grade of a test.

The Neocortex

The neocortex is the most modern part of the brain and the area where most dyslexia research is focused. Besides reading and writing, this upper-level part of the brain loves storytelling, puzzles, and organizational games, such as Lego and model airplane building. This modern brain can spin tales into the future and postulate what life might be like on another planet or in another time.

Interestingly, while both the reptilian brain and limbic system deal with outdoor life, the modern brain is most comfortable indoors. The neocortex is a bridge to abstract concepts, geometry (spatial concepts) built upon basic mathematics, and a sense of wonder. This modern brain is divided into left and right sides, and each side performs different functions. The whole brain functions best, of course, when the right and left sides work together in harmony.

The right brain flourishes with artistic expression, although fear and self-sabotage can lead to creative blocks early in life. Creative blocks and continued self-criticism keep the tender, vulnerable part of a person in hiding, afraid of being judged harshly. When creativity is stifled, the right brain becomes weak. Julie Cameron, author of *The Artist's Way,* helps adults overcome these creative blocks that often begin in childhood. The best part is that you don't need to be the least bit artistic to benefit from the principles she describes.

The left brain loves confronting mental challenges, deciphering codes, and mastering new materials. (Unfortunately, it is also where the judge or bully inside of you lives.) Reading, math, and linear or logical subjects are all left-brain functions, and tasks with which a dyslexic individual typically requires help. This help will not be effective, however, if treatment begins on the left side of the neocortex. Sadly, mainstream tutoring typically addresses only this area of the brain, while the truth is that the left brain will not be able to function at its best until all three levels of the brain (the reptilian brain, the limbic system, and the neocortex) are integrated and working optimally. You must deal with the reptilian brain, the limbic system, and then the right brain before tackling left-brain tasks.

"Our neocortex (rational brain) is so complex and powerful that through fear and overcontrol, it can interfere with the subtle restorative instinctual impulses and responses generated by the reptilian core," says Dr. Levine.[23] In other words, humans can talk themselves out of doing that which they instinctively know would be good for them. When routines such as spending too much time indoors and in front of a computer create a lopsided brain, learning suffers. Incorrect therapy can have a similiarly deleterious effect. When you treat the brain from the bottom up, the highest functions of the neocortex will blossom naturally.

CONCLUSION

The three brain boosters of exercise, play, and music can benefit not only dyslexics but also individuals with any type of learning disorder. Additionally, the options covered in this chapter can improve academic performance while also being just plain fun. They can increase brain function on an everyday basis and keep the spirit uplifted even in the face of difficult circumstances. Exercise, play, and music feed the brain and the soul.

Exercise helps the brain work faster. It improves memory, focus, and concentration. It spurs connections between the lowest and highest levels of the brain. It is no surprise that experts recommend performing any demanding mental tasks immediately after exercise.

Play is also essential. Play opens up access to all parts of the brain, allowing the individual to learn more easily. When stress shuts down the brain, play actually helps it heal, fostering creativity and upper-level brain function. It could be said that creative play keeps us close to our true selves.

Finally, music establishes the important sense of inner rhythm and stimulates the brain to become more coherent. Music calms and soothes the nervous system. It can quickly shift a person's mood in a more positive direction. Rhythm is crucial when learning how to read. Like exercise and play, music aids in the achievement of a well-rounded brain.

As you now know, all three parts of the brain need to be addressed and stimulated when reversing a learning disorder such as dyslexia. The reptilian brain learns through rhythm, routine, repetition, and ritual. The limbic system is activated and engaged through the act of caring for and feeling connected to human beings and other living things. The right side of the neocortex thrives on artistic freedom and expansive imagination, while the left brain appreciates linear, sequential, logical, and organized patterns. Only by dealing with these individual parts will the brain as a whole be rewired and learning problems reversed.

7.

Schooling, Tutoring, and Extracurricular Activities

When you are the parent of a learning-challenged child, sometimes it feels as though you are walking a tightrope. On one hand, you want to protect your child from the harshness of the outside world; on the other hand, you want your child to be a confident, independent member of society. Sending a child off to school can be a hard transition in the best of situations, but the process is even more nerve-wracking for families dealing with dyslexia or other similar learning conditions.

Your child may be a young adult preparing to attend college or a toddler who is soon to go to preschool. You may already be well aware of your child's dyslexia or you may have just learned of it recently. Regardless of the situation, you are no doubt facing a few fears in regard to your child's education. From public schools to private academies, there are a variety of options available to students. Learning about these options can help you find the best academic setting for your child. The brain begs to learn, and the process of learning may be optimized by matching your child's aptitudes and interests with a particular school.

In addition to different school settings, you may also be considering the usefulness of a tutor. Once you determine the reasons behind your child's poor grades and struggles with homework, tutoring may play an important role in solving these problems. Finding the best type of tutoring can be difficult, but the tips contained in this chapter can make the task an easier one.

Finally, extracurricular activities such as after-school clubs, team and individual sports, creative arts, and volunteering can enrich your child's life while also improving problem-solving and social skills. Like schools, these activities can be chosen based on your child's aptitudes and strengths.

Focus on Strengths

As you know, a decent level of self-esteem is integral to a child's ability and desire to learn. Instead of focusing only on the weaknesses of a learning-challenged child, it is important to focus on the strengths and engender a sense of pride. Sometimes, however, a child's strengths may not be so obvious, particularly when problems keep cropping up. If you don't know how your child learns best, seek out academic testing. If you don't have access to academic testing, you can buy informative books such as *Discover Your Child's Learning Style* by Mariaemma Willis and Victoria Kindle Hodson, which can help you and your child find the answers together. The assessment profiles contained in this book are geared to determine your child's disposition, talents, interests, and preferred learning modalities (visual, auditory, or kinesthetic) and environments. They even take into account a subject's temperament, eating habits, and energy levels throughout the day.

SCHOOLING

Between the ages of four and twenty-two, much of your child's schedule will revolve around schooling. From preschool to college, there will be numerous academic choices to make along the way. Learning can be hampered when an individual feels different or embarrassed, or is seen by others as a problem. Inasmuch as all children require a certain degree of confidence in order to succeed scholastically, a dyslexic child needs to feel particularly resilient and competent, and the right academic environment can foster these qualities.

Preschool

As discussed earlier, it is through touch that the human body learns how to judge distances—preliminary math, if you will. Proprioception—the sense that tells us where we are in relationship to other objects— is activated through touch and interaction with the environment. This tactile participation in the events of the outside world encourages the brain to map where sounds are coming from and where objects are located in relation to the body. These processes lay the foundation for proper learning. With this idea in mind, preschools that include lots of activities and physical movement, including play on the ground, can be of great benefit to children who display early signs of learning problems.

Elementary and Secondary Schools

When it comes to primary and secondary education, the main choice is between public and private schooling. Because children with learning conditions often benefit from a more tailor-made approach than they may find at a public school, the private option may sound like the most appropriate for your dyslexic child. Depending on where you live in the United States, however, there are certain public schools that offer specialized curricula. Known as magnet schools or academies, these institutions focus on a particular field of study, such as social sciences, performing arts, mathematics, or engineering. Magnet schools present a good option to children who display obvious strengths in certain areas.

Private schools, also called independent schools or non-state schools, rely on tuition rather than government funding. Private schools may be local, such as parochial schools, or they may require students to live away from home, as in the case of boarding schools. A private school may be geared towards particular learning challenges or other special needs. Military-type boarding schools—not to be confused with schools actually run by the military—may also provide a structure that is helpful to some children.

Depending on the focus of the school and its clientele, a child with learning differences may still thrive in the right school setting. It is important to note, however, that natural aptitudes may not become clear until the age of fourteen. Additionally, certain parts of the brain are accessed only between the ages of sixteen and the late twenties—a fact that may also make it difficult to ascertain which direction to choose for your child. Thankfully, in the United States, kids and adults can change course at any age. This advantage isn't available to everyone around the world.

Whether the school is private or public, a multisensory approach to learning will always be beneficial to a child with dyslexia. Ask any seasoned teacher how much practices such as marching, singing, and clapping, especially during the early school years, help children learn more easily. While these methods may be found in public schools, private Montessori schools and private Waldorf schools are known to encourage multisensory learning. As these two choices are not be available everywhere, or may be prohibitively expensive, charter schools and even homeschooling should also be considered when looking for a multisensory education.

Montessori Schools

Developed in the late nineteenth century by Italian physician and educator Maria Montessori, these schools are based on the belief that children have an inner wisdom. Given freedom and choice within a "prepared" Montessori environment, which includes multisensory learning, children are encouraged to develop independence and balance in their lives. There are approximately 4,500 Montessori-based schools in the United States. Some of them start shortly after birth and go through the age of eighteen. Most commonly, however, these schools go through the sixth grade.

Waldorf Schools

Created by Austrian Rudolf Steiner, the Waldorf approach to education can now be found in over 800 schools throughout the United States. Like Montessori, Steiner based his research on childhood and human development. Waldorf schools generally include children from kindergarten through the twelfth grade. The same teacher remains with a child for the first eight years of schooling. During the early years of Waldorf schooling, children spend a lot of time interacting with the environment outdoors. Through this method, they learn balance, near and far ocular focus, and how to get along with one another. Like the Danish school system, the Waldorf tradition does not introduce reading until the age of eight. Although classes follow the traditional grade structure, the child is encouraged to experience education through active participation, movement, and imagination. After working with many Waldorf children, I have seen firsthand how self-esteem is upheld in their whole-person approach.

Charter Schools

A charter school is publicly funded and typically governed by a group or organization under a legislative contract or charter with the state. On average, however, charter schools receive less funding than public schools, and they may receive private funding and foundation money. They have more freedom in curriculum design than most public schools and offer some innovative programs based on special interests. As of 2010, charter schools operate in forty states.

Whether a child has a better chance at succeeding at a charter school is up for debate. Statistics vary widely on which type of school is best, traditional or charter. The research and data-gathering designs differ so much that it is difficult to make a clear decision. This is no surprise really, because in 2009, a study from Stanford University compared 70 percent of charter school students with public school students in the same demographically matched areas. While 17 percent of charter school students scored significantly better than their public school counterparts, 46 percent showed no difference, and 37 percent did significantly worse.[1]

Homeschooling

Homeschooling can be a good choice if your child has trouble learning through traditional teaching styles. Keeping self-esteem intact is important, and for this reason alone many parents opt for homeschooling. Others prefer it because they can instill their own values in their children without interference from the school administration or society in general. Many parents who choose this option already have teaching degrees, but a degree isn't required to homeschool a child. Some parents

The Importance of Human Connection

We are wired to learn through interaction with our environment. We learn where we are spatially by judging distances, determining where sounds are coming from, and sensing where another person is located. We look people in the eye to see how they feel about something we said or did. The scary thing about various electronic media is that there is not a human being on the other end, so users miss the nuances and feedback involved in personal connection. Online video games include groups, but they do not offer true and complete social interaction, and they definitely do not qualify as exercise. We do children a disservice when we allow them too much pseudo-play and pseudo-connection via electronics.

Daniel Goleman's book *Emotional Intelligence* suggests that the ability to get along with others—our social and emotional intelligence—is hugely important to future success. Social skills come from interaction with other human beings. Honing these skills requires more than just emailing or texting friends; it requires eyeball-to-eyeball communication. Humans are complex creatures and need the full array of sensory interchange.

share teaching responsibilities by subject. For example, mom teaches math, dad teaches geography, and a neighbor or grandparent teaches another subject. Sometimes, parents who don't feel qualified to teach their children at home will hire a former teacher to do the job.

Socialization is a concern that often arises in connection with this version of learning. Many homeschooling organizations, of which there are hundreds, offer classes to cover certain subjects and make sure children have proper social outlets. Often homeschooled children will ease into a public or private school during their teenage years, when friends and peer relationships become very important.

Homeschooling is legal in all states, but details and laws vary considerably from district to district. The website www.hslda.org offers information on individual state laws.

Schools Not Recommended for Dyslexic Children

For children under the age of eight who have dyslexic tendencies, I do not recommend any school that emphasizes science and lacks art education. This approach does not honor the natural stages of brain development and can cause unnecessary problems. When children are asked to do tasks that they are not qualified or ready to do, they are likely to feel deficient, which is unfortunate, understandable, and just not true. Tummy aches, headaches, anxiety issues, and a lack of joy and spontaneity are just a few of the ways children's behavior may reflect this inner tension.

Colleges and Universities

Education beyond high school is available in many forms. A diagnosis of dyslexia does not mean your child won't succeed in a college setting; it does, however, mean you should consider schools and environments that will foster your child's strengths and tolerate your less desirable qualities.

For some students, the transition from high school to college-level academics begins early. Homeschoolers often take community college classes during the equivalent of their last two years of high school. Some charter school children also enroll in community college classes or take other classes online. Of course, public school kids are eligible to sign up for community college classes too, but their schedules may be less accommodating than those of their charter school or homeschooled counterparts.

College or University?

A college with small class sizes may be the right choice for those who might feel invisible in a typical university's introductory undergraduate courses of several hundred students. Local colleges are a good option, as they tend to be smaller than universities, allowing students to receive more attention than they might elsewhere, which may prevent them from falling through the cracks.

The move from high school to a university in another town away from family can be overwhelming, and many students drop out after the first semester. Living at home and attending a two-year junior college, or community college, is a comfortable solution for many young adults. This type of school offers associate degrees in a number of subjects, including certain vocational training programs. Students then have the option to transfer to a four-year institution to complete an undergraduate degree. The tuition and fees of a community college are usually lower than those of a bigger college or university. Tuition at private post-secondary institutions, which offer low student-teacher ratios, is often quite high. Community colleges also present an opportunity to explore several subjects without taking on too much of a financial burden.

Helpful Programs

Regardless of the type of higher education chosen, be sure to ask if the school extends special accommodations to people with special needs. Many dyslexics will do very well if allowed to approach a subject in creative ways. For example, some alternative colleges do not use the traditional grading system—a difference that can benefit those with learning difficulties.

Additionally, the AHEADD (Achieving in Higher Education) program (www.aheadd.org) can be extremely useful to individuals affected by various learning problems, including dyslexia and attention deficit disorder. Started in 2002, the AHEADD organization offers professional coaching and mentoring programs that support successful time management and organizational skills, use of school resources, and relationships with peers, professors, and school staff. AHEADD also provides families and school staff with training and support. If there is not an AHEADD group at a particular school or location, remote versions of this support program are available.

Another beneficial program is College Living Experience (www.experiencecle.com). This organization helps students with special needs acquire the academic and social skills that are essential to a successful college career, as well as the ability to manage their own living places while attending courses. College Living Experience offers year-round programs, which include individual case managers, academic liaisons, and mentors.

Other Options

Individuals who have dealt successfully with their dyslexia may not be interested in a traditional form of higher education. They may possess natural skills or aptitudes that can serve them in other ways. Vocational schools are designed for students who have graduated high school and wish to learn a trade such as automotive technology, carpentry, culinary arts, or aircraft maintenance engineering.

Many entrepreneurs have not completed college. In addition, 35 percent of entrepreneurs are considered dyslexic, and close to 70 percent of entrepreneurs claim to be affected by ADHD. Perhaps you've heard of Richard Branson, developer of Virgin Airlines; or Charles Schwab, the financial genius. They are among a long list of people who have accomplished much despite their learning challenges.

As a parent, your job is to find ways to let your learning-challenged child's deepest gifts and strengths to emerge—and these ways don't always include college, or any post-secondary school, for that matter. Be open to the path to which your child seems suited.

Aptitude Testing

For young adults considering college or any specialized vocational training, it might be wise to take an aptitude test before making a choice. The Johnson O'Connor Research Foundation (www.jocrf.org) provides aptitude testing for career and educational guidance. Adults who have taken this test tell me that the information it yielded was life changing. Parents of college-bound children often attest to the amazing accuracy of this testing method, explaining how it helped their children decide on an appropriate life path.

Aptitudes, it must be understood, are not necessarily interests. Interests can change from year to year as a result of life experience and exposure to outside influences. Aptitudes, on the other hand, have little to do with these external forces. They are innate, often inherited, and sometimes do not become apparent until around the age of fourteen.

TUTORING

Some parents have employed multiple tutors over many years, while other parents consider tutoring a crutch. When a tutor focuses only on teaching compensations, I agree with the latter. The goal should be building strength of character and increasing learning ability. Failing grades and homework struggles, however, are signs that a child needs help, and a good tutor can provide a valuable human connection and a reason to keep trying.

There are many possible reasons for poor academic performance, and it is important to ascertain the reason behind school troubles before hiring a tutor. It may not be a learning disorder. A personality conflict with a teacher, being bullied, internalized pressure to succeed, or even poor nutrition may be the cause of bad grades.

Once a learning disorder has been identified, finding the right tutor can be time consuming. So much will depend on your child's learning styles and strengths. If you go with a franchised learning center operation such as Sylvan, Huntington, or Kumon, there will be some level of standardization, which may or may not be helpful.

Tutoring may be done by computer program, one-on-one sessions, or small group sessions. Personally, I believe that children need one-on-one, eye-to-eye, heart-to-heart connections. Computers may augment sessions, but they are no substitute for human interaction, caring, and encouragement. By working with a tutor, students find not only the academic success that has eluded them for so long, but also a sense of self-validation that gives them confidence.

A neighbor, older brother or sister, or extended family member could also perform the duties of tutor. Senior citizens often have time to read to young children, and to listen to them read. If you are considering employing a tutor, the following tips may prove helpful.

Tutoring Tips

When it comes to finding a tutor, ask for recommendations everywhere. Interview a few different tutors and involve your child in the decision-making process. Children are more likely to cooperate with a tutor when they feel their opinions are valued. If you use a franchised learning center, request that your child have the same tutor each session once you've found a good fit. Finding the right match for your child is paramount. Just because a tutor helped the boy down the street doesn't mean that same tutor will be a good match for your child.

After checking your chosen tutor's references, try to schedule the sessions for a time when your child learns best. Right after school is the most common time for tutoring. Be sure to let your child have a snack and do some exercise before each session. Spot-check the tutoring practice by occasionally observing the process. There should be lots of interaction between tutor and child. I'm frequently taken aback when I see a child being tutored at a coffee shop or book store, sitting absentmindedly as the tutor explains concepts without making eye contact or encouraging interaction.

Just as successful bodybuilders must weight train several times a week, children with learning disorders need to attend more than one tutoring session a week if they wish to improve academically. Scheduling shorter but more frequent session increases repetition, which encourages better long-term myelination and a quicker speed of transmission within the brain. Children thrive on repetition and variation. Tutoring is not so different from learning a sport and going through the drills. You simply have to figure out the delivery style that is best for your child, and then find a tutor that fits this method.

Mentoring

Mentoring is a powerful way to bring out a child's potential. As aptitudes may be hereditary, perhaps a relative shares the same talents as your child. This family member could be a wonderful mentor. If a neighbor is involved in a particular field that is of interest to your child, perhaps this person could teach your child more about this subject. Perhaps you could locate a college professor who might mentor your child in the science lab.

I know of one very successful executive who had a lot of trouble in elementary school. Rather than spend money on tutors, his parents found a college professor who allowed him to become a junior lab assistant during the summers. The bond between child and professor lasted forty years, long after the mentoring relationship had provided a positive influence on the boy's future.

EXTRACURRICULAR ACTIVITIES

While schooling and tutoring are very important to a learning-challenged child's life, allowing exposure to various outside experiences and ideas is also vital. Many extracurricular programs enrich children's lives, and are probably available within a few miles of home. These activities can improve problem solving and social skills, and encourage special interests and hobbies. Extracurricular groups include Boy Scouts, Girl Scouts, 4-H club, chess clubs, theater groups, and volunteer groups at hospitals and places of worship.

Summer Activities

Summer camps and other social programs of the season can be very beneficial to a learning-challenged child. Camp is a fun way for kids to try out a variety of new activities. If your child shows a particular interest you'd like to encourage, specialized camps exist for almost any interest, including science and nature, puppetry, acting, art, writing, filmmaking, and even robotics. Camps may be found for a wide range of sports, including baseball or softball, tennis, golf, soccer, archery, cheerleading, gymnastics, and dance. While structured summer camps are great, helpful summer activities may also be quite informal. You could gather a few neighborhood kids and take turns with their parents organizing fun activities.

Additionally, many teens have the opportunity to visit other countries or participate in a volunteer project through their schools or religious groups. Seeing how other people live and what their values are can give children a new perspective on the world around them.

Year-round Activities

Various kinds of athletic programs may be available throughout the year in your community or through your child's school. Competitive games, where one team wins and another team loses, are not necessary; simply exercising the major muscle groups is the goal. Swimming, walking, jogging, and dancing are all great forms of exercise. Martial arts, tai chi, and acrobatics are great at teaching internal awareness and focus. Juggling is great for hand-eye coordination.

CONCLUSION

While schooling, tutoring, mentoring, and extracurricular activities all play vital roles in the successful future of any child, these different facets of education are even more crucial to the progress of someone with a learning disorder. When it comes to choosing schools, there are many options at each age level. Early education should include lots of physical movement and interaction with the environment. Once primary and secondary schools become part of the picture, try to figure out your child's learning style and aptitudes. It is important to learn your child's strengths and focus on them. Do not place too much emphasis on weaknesses. No one learns best by concentrating on their learning disorder. When it comes time for college, see if studies at any institutions match your child's aptitudes and interests. There are many post-secondary schools that allow students to focus on specific interests such as filmmaking, story writing, theater arts, and design.

There are other ways to improve a child's academic success, including those available outside the classroom. Tutoring may be very helpful if the tutor conveys a belief in your child's ability to succeed and excel, and deems your child's dyslexia to be a temporary condition. In addition, finding a mentor for your child can be beneficial. A strong relationship with a mentor can increase positive feelings and particular skill sets.

Finally, extracurricular activities expose children to new experiences and ideas, allowing creativity to flow. Playing a sport is an easy way to get exercise, which, as you know, stimulates neural connections and primes the brain to learn more quickly and easily. Extracurricular groups also provide a sense of human connection and belonging, which create the feeling of safety and encourage the ability to learn.

Yes, there are ideal times to create channels within the brain and body that are necessary for various kinds of learning. It is still possible, however, to undo misaligned connections and rewire the brain and body after these ideal times have passed. New scientific breakthroughs continue to prove this fact. Although we know enough to turn our previous understanding of learning upside down, we are still at the beginning stages of understanding what is truly possible. With the right approach, most individuals with learning disorders can attain college diplomas or vocational certificates and be quite successful.

I have seen many clients of mine successfully achieve degrees and certifications in many fields. I have worked with adults who went on to attain law degrees, medical degrees, dental degrees, and teaching degrees in spite of their dyslexia. Persistence and the right perspective can lead to a remarkable outcome.

Conclusion

At this point, I hope you understand why the problem of dyslexia remains such a riddle, and how mainstream treatment, at best, relies mostly on teaching compensatory techniques. Hopefully, you also recognize that there really is a genuine reason to believe in the possibility of rewiring the brain and reversing dyslexia, allowing resilience and strength to replace fear and anxiety. Sharon Begley, brain researcher and author, sums up what science has slowly begun to confirm by stating, "We can't control the brain we're born with, but we can control the brain we end up with."[1] In other words, dyslexics can absolutely have a future without this learning disorder. Whether you seek to treat your child or yourself, know that you are the true catalyst for this amazing transformation.

If you have a child with dyslexia, I hope this book has empowered you to stand up and become an advocate for change, armed with all the scientifically based reasons why dyslexia is reversible. This book aims to provide you with the tools and resources to achieve real and positive results. With this new information and vocabulary at your disposal, you can now challenge authorities who insist your child play by the same old rules. You may seek new avenues of treatment and make lifestyle adjustments that will benefit not only your dyslexic child but also your whole family.

According to renowned educational psychologist Dr. Jane M. Healy, "When children all over the world were asked about the most important ingredient for their well-being, they overwhelmingly named their families."[2] This can be both a soothing and scary thought. At first, the best way to help your dyslexic child is to stop blaming yourself for the problem. It is also beneficial to stop worrying that you are not capable of solving this issue. Move away from this entire mindset. The fact that you are reading this book is evidence that you are taking the right steps for your child and yourself.

Even in the face of dyslexia, you have the power to help your child achieve a winning attitude towards life. But raising a child, of course, is no spectator sport. It's a roll-up-your-shirt-sleeves endeavor. This book is not simply meant to get you and your family on the winning team, it is meant to create a whole new playing field —one on which your child will find success. The former rules about school and learning no longer apply. This is a new era, and our understanding of how we learn needs to be updated. You no longer have to stand back, watch your child suffer, and feel helpless. There is help and there is hope.

Remember that you are the overseer of your child's blueprint, and you can help your child become a mighty fortress with a solid foundation. This is an overwhelming reality, but a good one. In spite of endless rules and regulations, when it comes to your child, you are still the one with the power to change the situation—and the most important power you possess is love. Your love and support help satisfy the basic and emotional needs of the brain. When a child does not feel safe or cared for, any learning that actually takes place is simply a fortunate luxury. Wealth, toys, and fancy clothes, however, have nothing to do with creating a sense of warmth and safety for a child.

The creation of a safe and supportive home that allows your child's brain the freedom to learn begins by establishing routines. Remember, the reptilian brain thrives and is comforted by four things: routine, ritual, repetition, and rhythm. Is there a daily rhythm and routine in your household? Getting up at the same time, going to bed at the same time, and having meals at the same time all count towards calming your child's nervous system. Children love to know their limits and how far can they push you. They unknowingly beg for boundaries, and they need to know what they can expect and count on from their parents.

While it is important to engage in activities as a family, be sure to make time for one-on-one bonding with your dyslexic child on a regular basis. This quality time is precious to both parent and child. Leave your worries and thoughts at the door. Just be there—totally there—with your child. This kind of experience will build up a bank account of treasured memories for your child to hold near when times get rough. A particularly great way to bond and create memories is through music, so listen to or make up catchy songs with your child. Different kinds of music can elicit different kinds of moods. Find music you and your child would like to hear while doing creative projects, relaxing, or just focusing quietly. Definitely make a point to play a few songs that make you and your child feel like jumping for joy and having fun.

Of course, do not be inflexible about routines. If a change in your typical daily plan is necessary, tell your child about it ahead of time and explain what will be going on for the day. Children feel empowered and important when they are made part of the discussion.

Remember to point out your dyslexic child's strengths. Take time to notice what your child does well naturally and then encourage these inborn talents. Give specific compliments ("I like how you stuck with your project even when you might have wanted to quit," for example) instead of vague, generalized ones ("You are so smart"). Reinforce persistence, but emphasize curiosity instead of letter grades. Encourage problem solving and recognize the attempt. When your child makes a valiant effort, reinforce this effort, not necessarily the outcome. Focus on free play rather than structured, competitive games, and always be generous with your hugs. Be helpful in every way you can, but also be careful not to do everything for your child; it weakens the spirit.

Although learning disorders can make life difficult, stop yourself from speaking when angry. The words that come out of your mouth will be coming from a reactive place and probably not a kind one. The old saying about sticks and stones is utterly untrue. Angry words can and do hurt children, and echo in the psyche for years. Be a model of good decision making and self-control. Display consideration of others and teach your child to establish boundaries. Keep in mind, however, that there is no magic spell to turn you into a perfect parent overnight. Consistency over time builds assurance in children. Just as there is no magic parenting spell, there is also no quick fix to create a resilient, successful child. It is only through a parent's diligence and sustained effort that a child's life may be changed for the better.

Understandably, when you are the parent of a dyslexic child, it is easy to forget to address your own needs. While ignoring your own well-being may sound like a noble thing to do, it is actually a big mistake. If you do not deal with your own needs in one way or another, you may not be able to recognize or meet the needs of your child. I know that determining your own needs can seem impossible, and that doing something about them can seem even more so. There is one requirement, however, that all parents have in common: reducing stress.

But how can you reduce your stress levels when most days are so hard? To answer this question, ask yourself the following: Do you take any time for yourself to center and set a good tone for the day? Some parents get up fifteen minutes earlier than the rest of the family to have "quiet time." During that time, they may stare blankly while drinking a cup of coffee. Some meditate, others read affirmations or a meaningful book, and still others get out their "to do" lists and organize the day. Finding your center may be the most important task you face all day.

Additionally, don't forget that exercise is a great stress releaser and helps keep you on an even keel. The same goes for a healthful diet, quality sleep patterns, and social connections. If you don't have anyone to talk to, find someone—anyone. You'll be amazed by how helpful the simple act of getting something of your chest can be.

Now that you know how to take charge of your life and the life of your child, my dream is that you take this knowledge and pay it forward. My hope is that you will join hands with other parents who need encouragement and hope for their children. Parents need each other, and children need parents to be strong and available. Share information with other parents. Form small groups to converse with each other. Start a blog about your experience. Just start speaking up about the idea of reversing dyslexia. Empowered, you can now be a role model to your children and other parents. If you have the financial resources, put your money where your mouth is. Invest in getting new therapies into the mainstream through the validation of good research. Donate to studies on neuroplasticity and epigenetics, and give to alternative therapy programs in your town and elsewhere.

Take dyslexia out of the shadows. It does not need to be seen as a horrible problem because, in most cases, it doesn't have to be a permanent condition; it's reversible. It isn't anything to be ashamed of, and it's nothing to feel guilty about. Denial and an unquestioned belief in out-of-date information are perpetuating a false view of dyslexia and other learning disorders. Sadly, dyslexic children often experience emotional trauma from the idea that they must be the problem, that they are irrevocably flawed. This opinion, of course, just isn't true, and it is a thought process that must stop.

Please take what you know and change the popular mindset. Dyslexics are often brilliant in ways other people simply fail to recognize. Successful dyslexics learn how to delegate, how to accept the fact that things might not come easily, and how to think outside the box. These are all great traits that not everyone learns. The goal of this book is to maintain these good qualities while allowing the dyslexic individual access to a fully integrated brain.

"Nothing happens to us; it happens for us," is a phrase I live by. Dyslexia is not an insurmountable obstacle, although I know it can seem like a huge boulder standing in the way of a successful life. When we persevere, good things happen. Don't give up on your child or yourself. You have the answer to the riddle; do not hesitate to speak it out loud.

References

Chapter Two

1. Hüther, Gerald. *The Compassionate Brain: How Empathy Creates Intelligence*. Boston: Trumpeter, 2006.

2. Panksepp, Jaak. *Affective Neuroscience: The Foundations of Human and Animal Emotions*. New York: Oxford University Press, 2004.

3. Bowers, Brent. "Study Shows Stronger Link Between Entrepreneurs and Dyslexia." *New York Times* 5 Nov. 2007.

Chapter Three

1. MacLean, Paul. *The Triune Brain in Evolution: Role in Paleocerebral Functions*. New York: Springer, 1990.

2. Pearce, Joseph Chilton. *The Biology of Transcendence: A Blueprint of the Human Spirit*. Rochester, VT: Park Street Press, 2002.

Chapter Four

1. Lipton, Bruce H. *Biology of Belief: Unleashing the Power of Consciousness, Matter & Miracles*. Carlsbad, CA: Hay House, 2005.

2. Doidge, Norman. *The Brain That Changes Itself: Stories of Personal Triumph from the Frontiers of Brain Science*. New York: Penguin Books, 2007.

3. Ibid.

4. Walker, Jonathan, and Charles Norman. "The Neurophysiology of Dyslexia: A Selective Review with Implications for Neurofeedback Remediation and Results of Treatment in Twelve Consecutive Patients." *Journal of Neurotherapy* 2006; 10(1):45—55.

5. Ratey, John. *Spark: The Revolutionary New Science of Exercise and the Brain.* New York: Little, Brown & Company, 2013.

Chapter Five

1. Milne, Hugh. *The Heart of Listening: A Visionary Approach to Cranial Sacral Work.* Berkeley, CA: North Atlantic Books, 1995.

2. Pollan, Michael. *In Defense of Food: An Eater's Manifesto.* New York: Penguin Press, 2008.

Chapter Six

1. Ratey, John. *Spark: The Revolutionary New Science of Exercise and the Brain.* New York: Little, Brown & Company, 2008.

2. Ibid.

3. "Nearly Third of Children Are Couch Potatoes." *Reuters Life* 29 March. 2010.

4. Reynolds, Gretchen. "Phys Ed: Can Exercise Make Kids Smarter?" *New York Times* 17 Sept. 2010.

5. Ibid.

6. Ibid.

7. Hannaford, Carla. *Smart Moves: Why Learning Is Not All in Your Head.* Salt Lake City, UT: Great Rivers Books, 2005.

8. Panksepp, Jaak. *Affective Neuroscience: The Foundations of Human and Animal Emotions.* New York: Oxford University Press, 2004.

9. Ibid.

10. Hannaford, Carla. *Playing in the Unified Field: Raising & Becoming Conscious, Creative Human Beings.* Salt Lake City, UT: Great Rivers Books, 2010.

11. Blythe, Sally Goddard. *The Well Balanced Child: Movement and Early Learning.* Stroud, UK: Hawthorne Press, 2005.

12. Ibid.

13. Ibid.

14. Deasy, Richard J., ed. *Critical Links: Learning in the Arts and Student Academic and Social Development.* Washington, D.C.: Arts Education Partnership, 2002.

15. Anvari, Sima H, et al. "Relations Among Musical Skills, Phonological Processing and Early Reading Ability in Preschool Children." *Journal of Experimental Child Psychology* 2002 Oct; 83(2):111—130.

16. Rauscher, Frances H. *Can Music Instruction Affect Children's Cognitive Development?* Champaign, IL: ERIC Clearinghouse on Early Education and Parenting, 2003.

17. Hansen, Dee, and Bernstorf, E. "Linking Music Learning to Reading Instruction." *Music Educators Journal* 2002 Mar; 88(5):17—21.

18. Campbell, Don. *The Mozart Effect: Tapping the Power of Music to Heal the Body, Strengthen the Mind and Unlock the Creative Spirit.* New York: Harper Collins, 2009.

19. McCormick, A. and Marlena McCormick. *Horse Sense and the Human Heart: What Horses Can Teach Us About Trust, Bonding, Creativity and Spirituality.* Deerfield Beach, Fl.: Health Communications, 1997.

20. Dossey, Larry. "The Healing Power of Pets: A Look at Animal-Assisted Therapy." *Altern Ther Health Med* 2007 Jul; 3(4):8—16.

21. Levine, Peter A. *Waking the Tiger: Healing Trauma.* Berkeley, CA: North Atlantic Books, 1997.

22. Goleman, Daniel. *Emotional Intelligence: Why It Can Matter More Than IQ.* New York: Bantam, 2006.

23. Levine, Peter A. *Waking the Tiger: Healing Trauma.* Berkeley, CA: North Atlantic Books, 1997.

Chapter Seven

l. Chen, Grace. "Charter Schools or Traditional Public Schools: Which One Is Underperforming?" *Public School Review* 10 Jul. 2009.

Conclusion

1. Begley, Sharon, and Ruth Buczynski. *National Institute for the Clinical Application of Behavioral Medicine.* Interview Apr 13. 2012.

2. Healy, Jane. *Different Learners: Identifying, Preventing and Treating Your Child's Learning Problems.* New York: Simon & Schuster, 2011.

About the Author

Phyllis Books, DC, CCN, holds a BA in education and English from Michigan State University, a master's degree in education and interpersonal communication from the University of North Texas, and a doctorate of chiropractic from Parker University in Dallas, Texas. She is also a Certified Clinical Nutritionist. Since 1986, she has specialized in pediatrics and learning differences.

Dr. Books is a highly sought-after lecturer and workshop educator. She is also the founder of Books Neural Therapy, an integrative, multidisciplinary system designed to improve the neurological, emotional, and chemical issues implicated in learning disorders. She heads the Books Family Health Center in Austin, Texas, and recently released the world's first online Dyslexia Reversal System class. When she isn't with her clients, teaching, or lecturing, you might find her pitching a baseball or building forts with her grandchildren.

Index

Socialization skills
    exercise as tool for improving, 96
    extracurricular activities as
        tools for improving, 125
    importance of, for learning,
        118–119
    media use as detriment to, 118
    play as tool for improving, 101
Spatial intelligence, music as tool
    for improving, 105
SPD. *See* Sensory Processing
    Disorder.
Sports
    benefits of, to social skills, 96,
        125
    injuries, learning impaired by, 16
SSS. *See* Scotopic Sensitivity
    Syndrome.
Sugar
    alternative names for, 88–89
    alternatives to, 81–82
    American consumption of, 81
    as detriment to learning, 17–20
    impairment of vision, reading,
        due to intake of, 18–19, 80
Summer camps, benefits of, 125
Suzuki method, 106
Television usage. *See* Media
    usage.
Thinking brain. *See* Neocortex.
Tomatis Method, 62
Touch for Health, 60
Treatment, what to expect during,
    71–72. *See also* Dyslexia,
    treatments of.

Triune Brain model, 40–49
    communication between
        components of, 49
    limbic system in, 41, 45, 107–109
    neocortex in, 41–42, 46–47,
        109–110
    reptilian brain in, 41–42, 69, 107
Tutoring
    franchises, value of, 123
    mentoring versus, 124
    one-on-one style of, 123
    scheduling and creating proper
        environment for, 124
Vestibular system, 43
Video game usage. *See* Media
    usage.
Vision Therapy, 63–64
Visual processing,
    impairment of, 8–9
    impairment of, due to sugar
        intake, 19, 80
    treatments for improving, 61,
        63–64
Visual Theory, 8–9
Vocational school, 121
Waldorf schools, 117
Water, importance of, 84
Wheat, 78–79
    gluten-free alternatives to, 79,
        87
    health problems arising from,
        78
Withdrawal, emotional, 31–32
Young, Barbara Arrowsmith,
    52–53

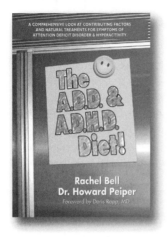

THE A.D.D. & A.D.H.D. DIET!

Rachel Bell and Howard Peiper, ND

In this book, authors Rachel Bell and Dr. Howard Peiper take a uniquely nutritional approach to treating ADD and ADHD. After addressing the causes of the disorders, from poor nutrition and food allergies to environmental contaminants, the authors discuss which foods your child can eat and which foods he should avoid. To make changing your child's diet easier, the authors also offer their very own healthy and delicious recipes. Final chapters examine the importance of detoxifying the body, supplementing diet with vitamins and nutrients, and exercising regularly.

$10.95 US • 112 pages • 6 x 9-inch quality paperback • ISBN 978-1-884820-29-8

THE IRLEN REVOLUTION

A Guide to Changing Your Perception and Your Life

Helen Irlen

After decades of revolutionizing the treatment of dyslexia through the use of colored lenses, educational pioneer Helen Irlen has turned her attention to children and adults who suffer from other learning disabilities. *The Irlen Revolution* examines the author's unique program for helping people with ADHD/ADD, Asperger's syndrome, autism, depth perception problems, head injuries, strokes, and a host of other conditions that affect learning.

$17.95 US • 224 pages • 6 x 9-inch quality paperback • ISBN 978-0-7570-0236-6

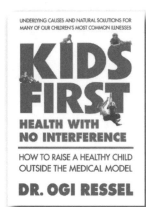

KIDS FIRST

Health with No Interference

Ogi Ressel, DC

Designed for parents, teachers, health professionals, and all who share in the care of children, *Kids First: Health with No Interference* helps you determine the underlying causes of many children's illnesses and assists you in creating a healing program that will produce lasting results.

$16.95 US • 272 pages • 6 x 9-inch quality paperback • ISBN 978-0-9701110-8-1

HOW TO MAXIMIZE YOUR CHILD'S LEARNING ABILITY

A Complete Guide to Choosing and Using the Best Computer Games, Activities, Learning Aids, Toys, and Tactics for Your Child

Lauren Bradway, PhD, and Barbara Albers Hill

Over twenty years ago, Dr. Lauren Bradway discovered that all children use one of three distinct ways to grasp and remember informa- tion. Some learn best through visual stimula- tion; others, through sound and language; and others, through touch. In this unique book, Dr. Bradway first shows you how to determine your child's inherent style. She then aids you in carefully selecting the toys, activities, and educational strategies that will help reinforce the talents your child was born with, and encourage those skills that come less easily.

$14.95 US • 288 pages • 6 x 9-inch quality paperback • ISBN 978-0-7570-0096-6